Prophetic V

Peace

A Jewish, Christian and Humanist

Primer on

Colonialism, Zionism and

Nationalism in the Middle East

Prophetic Voices on Middle East Peace

A Jewish, Christian and Humanist Primer

on Colonialism, Zionism and Nationalism in

the Middle East

Thomas E. Phillips

Peter J. Miano

&

Jason Mitchell, editors

CLAREMONT STUDIES IN
CONTEMPORARY ISSUES

Prophetic Voices on Middle East Peace
A Jewish, Christian and Humanist Primer on
Colonialism, Zionism and Nationalism in the Middle
East

©2016 Claremont School of Theology Press
1325 N. College Ave
Claremont, CA 91711

ISBN 978-0692774854

Library of Congress Cataloging-in-Publication Data

Prophetic Voices on Middle East Peace: A Jewish,
Christian and Humanist Primer on Colonialism,
Zionism and Nationalism in the Middle East / edited
by Thomas E. Phillips, Peter J. Miano & Jason Mitchell
      p. cm. –(Claremont Studies in Contemporary
      Issues)
      Includes bibliographical references and
      index.
      ISBN 978-0692774854
      Subjects: 1. Jewish-Arab Relations—Religious
Aspects 2. Zionism 3. Peace—Religious Aspects

Call Number: DS119.76 .P45 2016

Dedicated to the victims of nationalism, colonialism and violence across the globe and across the ages

Table of Contents

Preface

This volume arose out of the passion and organizational skills of Rev. Peter Miano, executive director of the Society for Biblical Studies. For over two decades, Rev. Miano has led pilgrimages, organized conferences and advocated for peace and justice in the Holy Lands. The contributors to this volume were recruited by Rev. Miano to offer oral presentations at a conference sponsored by the Society for Biblical Studies (*Christians and the Holy Land: What Does the Lord Require?* on September 17–19, 2015, in Lexington, MA). Because the speakers were so eminently qualified, the prose so passionate and eloquent and the topic so immensely important, the speakers were invited to contribute their addresses for dissemination to a broader audience through this publication.

The process of moving from oral performance to written discourse can be challenging—even for seasoned orators and skilled writers like the contributors to this volume. Rather than editing away the power of their spoken words, the editors decided to preserve as much of the character of the original oral presentations as possible, complete with their shortened—often fragmentary—sentences, their signs of audible emphasis and their often non-standard syntax, grammar, idioms and punctuation. Such informalities should not distract the reader from the substance and passion of this discourse. The contributors are distinguished scholars and careful thinkers, but within this volume they speak as prophets of justice, and not merely as detached academics.

In most cases, the content of these essays arise from years—even decades—of careful study and observation. The contributors' published works, partially listed in the bibliography of this volume, well illustrate the typically meticulous character of their research. However, much of the documentation and scholarly apparatus normally associated with their scholarship has been abbreviated in this volume to avoid distractions. Readers who are interested in pursuing the literary and research trails behind the contributors' essays are invited to read the authors' other published works. (Most of the oral presentations were heavily dependent upon the authors' more traditional scholarly publications.) In some cases, the editor has added documentation to the authors' original manuscripts. These editorial supplements are clearly marked by an asterisk.* The web addresses for open-access resources have often been provided in the footnotes, although only print resources and versions are included in the bibliography.

Forward

Ralph Waldo Emerson once said, "A foolish consistency is the hobgoblin of little minds." (1841, "Self Reliance," *Essays: First Series*) Much public discourse about Israel and Palestine displays such foolish consistency. Politicians, pundits and a myriad of voices that influence public policy adopt and pass on unexamined, ideologically driven opinions not only with predictable regularity, but also with remarkable nonchalance. The result is that in the popular imagination in the United States, the Zionist narrative, with its various canards, is regarded as "canonical." For some, any suggestion that the elements of the Zionist narrative be subjected to normal, academic critique is viewed as heretical. Public discourse in the United States about Israel and Palestine is stunted. In light of the central position in public policy occupied by the relationship between United States and Israel, such consistency in opinion is not merely unbecoming. It is tragic. An eminently solvable problem with global implications is perpetuated largely due to the rigid adherence to uncritically accepted canards.

The essays in this volume were presented at the conference *Christians and the Holy Land: What Does the Lord Require?* The purpose of the conference was to present sub-dominant views and in so doing to correct the monotonous consistency in public discourse on the Israeli-Palestinian conflict. The speakers presented views that are not normally included in either mainstream media or general Church discourse. These perspectives are usually ignored, deliberately suppressed or otherwise unknown in critical discourse, in the mainstream media and in general lay conversation. This is because they fall outside of, or diverge from, the boundaries of the dominant, canonical narrative of the Israeli-Palestinian conflict. This unresolved conflict not only effects millions of people in, and well beyond, the Middle East, including Europe and the United States, it also involves millions of people in supporting and perpetuating the conflict. These include those who design and implement political, economic and ideological support for the Zionist enterprise. It includes politicians, critical scholars, those who shape public opinion and those who formulate their own opinions based on information gleaned from others.

As the subtitle of this volume suggests and as the dedication reminds us, Zionism is properly associated with both colonialism and nationalism. As Dr. Phillips states in his introduction, "...Zionism is not Judaism." We insist on that distinction and propose that Zionism be considered as another form of nationalism subject to the same critique as all nationalist ideology.

Although nationalism is a relatively recent historical phenomenon, unheard of prior to very late in the 18th century, very few can imagine a world organized in any way other than in the categories of nationalism: distinct territorial dimensions (i.e., national boundaries), the idea of *peoplehood* based primarily on simple language affinity, and national/state apparatus dedicated to preserving the privilege of parochial and imagined ethnic groups that share the perception of a common culture. While the emergence of nationalist identities over the past 200 years has been accompanied by nationalist warfare on an historically unprecedented level, few examine the practicality, let alone the morality of the nationalist enterprise. Colonization, with its assumptions of ethnic, racial and cultural supremacy and with its deliberate exclusivity is so closely associated with European and North American nationalism that it is tempting to consider them inseparable. The well documented brutality of all nationalist/colonialist enterprises, including the many varieties of genocide that they entail, requires careful reexamination of the relationship between nationalism and colonialism and our collective complicity in both. This reexamination should occur in practical, political and, perhaps most appropriately, moral terms. In the case of Western nationalism and colonization, the complicity of the Church and Church people in legitimating nationalist, colonialist projects renders this reexamination a moral and theological imperative.

Zionism is a strain of nationalism, although no significant historical phenomenon can be distilled to one, single, simple concept. No less than other nationalist movements, Zionism, among other things, is a settler, colonialist project. Since it enjoys a singular connection to a biblical land and employs a direct appeal to a biblical narrative of privilege and Divine legitimation, Zionism invites critical and moral examination as much as, if not more so, than other nationalist projects. Our work as biblical scholars and students of the Bible, especially when we work up close and personally in the holy lands with people of all faiths and many nationalities, requires us to engage the obvious and undeniable challenges of historical, biblical and moral critique. As ones who explicitly and conscientiously claim the biblical narrative as our own, our examination is not merely an academic one, but is part and parcel with our ecclesiastical, spiritual and moral obligations.

The biblical faith is spiritually redemptive only when it is politically engaged, socially responsible and morally relevant. We present the essays included in this volume in the hope that we will broaden the discourse, deepen understanding and assist the reader in his or her own spiritual and moral development.

Rev. Peter J. Miano
The Society for Biblical Studies
Arlington, Mass

Introduction

Having been engaged in leading pilgrimages to the holy lands for more than 15 years, we (Rev. Miano and Dr. Phillips) have become accustomed, sadly, to hearing the same familiar litany of questions from would-be pilgrims to these truly sacred, but tragically scarred, lands. "Is it safe to travel over there?" "Do you think there will ever be peace over there?" "Why can't they all just 'get along' over there?" "They've been fighting for thousands of years over there."

Of course, sometimes we encounter would-be travelers—or even veterans of commercial holy land tours—who shed the pretense of inquiry and simply lay bare the unstated assumptions behind the questions offered by others. People often assert, with an air of deep self-assurance, that "there will never be peace in the Middle East," or "the Arabs will never allow the Jews to live in peace," or, with more than a tinge of theological naiveté, "only Christ can bring peace to the holy land."

Such familiar refrains are as misguided as they are common. In this volume, a panel of distinguished scholars, analysts and activists speak as Jews, Christians and Humanists to name and explore the chief barriers to peace and stability in the holy lands.[1] These barriers are: nationalism, colonialism and Zionism.

In the opening chapter, Sara Roy speaks as a Jew and as a child of Holocaust survivors and draws parallels between the Nazi project to marginalize and then to extinguish Jewish culture and the Zionist project to marginalize and extinguish the Arab presence in the Israel, Gaza and the West Bank. Although Dr. Roy is clear that the Nazi project and the Zionist project are different in scale and ferocity, she argues that both projects are rooted in a shared sense of cultural superiority and disregard for the other. Dr. Roy asserts that contemporary Israeli policy toward the Palestinians betrays the core values of the Judaism that she learned as the child of Holocaust survivors.

---

[1] Unfortunately, the serendipity of academic schedules, conference timing and American visa restrictions made it impossible to include any of the myriad of peace-loving Muslim prophetic voices within these proceedings. We consider this lacuna an obvious defect. The voices of prophetic Muslims are routinely, obviously and deliberately suppressed in popular discourse about Israel and Palestine, especially in the American context. Our conference was, and this volume is, incomplete without them.

In the second chapter, Mark Braverman also speaks as a morally sensitive Jew, comparing Zionism to the Apartheid tradition in South Africa. Dr. Braverman locates Jesus within the prophetic tradition of Judaism and suggests that both the prophetic tradition of the Hebrew Bible and the teachings of Jesus in the Gospels challenge an exclusivist understanding of the people of God. Therefore, in light of his understanding of both Jesus' teaching and the prophetic tradition, Braverman calls for the church, the chief enabler of the Zionist project, to follow the example of the Christian leaders who helped to bring an end to Apartheid in South Africa by declaring that racist system to be heretical and counter to the Christian faith.

The volume's third chapter is also composed by a Jewish thinker, in fact, an Israeli citizen, Dr. Ilan Pappe. Based upon his experience as an Israeli observer of daily life in Israel/Palestine, Pappe argues that activists, intellectuals and policy makers should change the language they employ when discussing the situation in Israel/Palestine. He argues that Zionism should be labeled as a colonial project, that the segregation of Israelis and Palestinians should be described as Apartheid and that Israeli efforts to dislocate and marginalize Arab populations

3

should be regarded as ethnic cleansing. Pappe argues that the wide-scale use of these linguistically appropriate designations is a prerequisite to any significant movement toward policy changes within Israel and toward a just and lasting peace.

In the fourth chapter, Stephen Walt speaks as a policy analyst and offers a stinging (nonpartisan) critique of American policies toward the Middle East since World War II. Dr. Walt asserts that one persistent mistake (among the many other mistakes) has been the United States' tendency to maintain special relationships with a few Middle Eastern nations, Israel most prominently. Dr. Walt argues that the US should take a much less active role in promoting the interests of a selective group of nations and should instead treat all Middle Eastern nations consistently, evaluating the various nations on the basis of human rights and American interests—not "special relationships." Walt insists that Israel's treatment of the Palestinians within both Israel and Palestine should not be exempt from ethical critique by US policy makers.

The fifth chapter, the keynote address for the conference, contains Noam Chomsky's assessment of the Iranian nuclear deal that was negotiated in 2015. Chomsky, a Humanist with Jewish ancestry, argues that

4

there are certain facts, policy assumptions and ethical considerations that are being exempted from sustained moral inquiry by policy makers. Most importantly, Chomsky criticizes the rampant nationalism within the American context. Chomsky sees the assumption of American exceptionalism, and its stepchild of Israeli nationalism (Zionism), as tremendous impediments to any just and lasting peace with Iran and throughout the Middle East.

The sixth chapter moves to the Christian tradition and heeds the voice of Jean Zaru, the only female Church leader in Israel and Palestine. Ms. Zaru is a Palestinian Quaker who lives in the West Bank and who works as a peace activist in that context. Ms. Zaru offers a compelling personal account of her struggle to maintain hope and optimism under permanent military occupation. As a Quaker, Ms. Zaru (like most Palestinians) is committed to nonviolent change. In spite of the legacy of Israeli occupation and oppression, Ms. Zaru promotes the vision of a peaceful, inclusive and prosperous land where adherents of all faiths live together with common human rights.

In the final chapter, Rev. Peter Miano examines what he calls mainstream Christian Zionism. Miano argues that Christians should be deeply engaged in the moral critique of Zionism because Zionism is a greater phenomenon within Christianity than it is within Judaism. He notes that there are more Christian Zionists than there are Jewish Zionists—and he notes that Zionism is not merely a phenomenon of fundamentalist and dispensational Christianity. Zionism is also a mainstream Christian phenomenon. Miano, therefore, argues that mainstream Christian thinkers should analyze the moral dimensions of Zionism within their own Christian tradition.

The topic within this volume is controversial; the rhetoric is often strong. It is the hope of this volume that peace in the holy lands can be invigorated by the collective courage of Jews, Christians and Humanists[1] who join together to speak prophetically—even when those prophetic voices utter some harsh truths.

As the editors see it, one set of harsh truths is quite simple:

- The segregation and oppression of an entire class of people on the bases of religion and ethnicity can only be maintained by gross violations of human rights.
- Israeli policies, as informed by a Zionist ideology, promote and enforce the segregation and oppression of an entire class of people on the bases of religion and ethnicity.

6

- Israeli (Zionist) policies can only be maintained by gross violations of human rights.
- Peace and justice cannot be maintained in the face of such gross violations of human rights.
- The pursuit of peace and justice in the holy lands begins with the abolition of Zionism.

Of course, the acknowledgement of these truths in no way implies an end to the cherished, revered and sacred traditions and practices of Judaism. May God bless the Jewish people and the Jewish faith, but Zionism is not Judaism. May God banish all forms of racism, colonialism, exceptionalism and self-aggrandizing nationalism to the historical waste basket to which they belong. May God bless the peoples—all the peoples—of the holy lands! May justice and righteousness flow from the hills like a river to all people. May we seek justice and the promotion of human rights without exceptions, exemptions or special pleading.

Thomas E. Phillips

Gaza
A Reflection

Sara Roy

Before this conference Rev. Peter Miano sent me an article that criticized this conference and some of its speakers. Among the comments made were these: "Another speaker, Sara Roy from Harvard University, has drawn parallels between Israeli soldiers and Nazis who murdered Jews during Germany's Third Reich. There's also a representative from 'Breaking the Silence,' a group of former IDF soldiers who level unsubstantiated allegations at their erstwhile comrades."[1]

Over the last 30 years of research and writing on the Israeli-Palestinian conflict, I have been accused

---

[1] Dexter Van Zile, "Truth Not a Requirement at Methodist Church's Upcoming Anti-Israel Conference," *JNS.org News Service* (September 7, 2015). Available online at: www.jns.org/latest-articles/2015/9/7/truth-not-a-requirement-at-methodist-churchs-upcoming-anti-israel-conference#.VikWFCiRs2A (accessed 5/16/16).*

of many terrible things—as have all of the presenters here—but such attacks do raise crucial questions about the relationship between scholarship and politics in writing about the Israeli-Palestinian conflict, the writer's moral and political responsibility, and how the writer came to his or her position. I would like to address these issues using Gaza as my mirror. I also will take you on my own personal journey.

On Partisanship, or Whom I Represent

Among the many themes that demand to be addressed, I shall begin by focusing on just two: *partisanship* or *whom I represent* and the *nature of dissent*.

Let's begin with the issue of partisanship. The gross lack of objectivity, which the journalist I just quoted would no doubt accuse me of, involves, among other things, the issue of whom I represent. The common response, of course, is that I represent the Palestinian side as an advocate or polemicist. This answer reduces 30 years of study, research, and analysis to mere ideological positioning. I have never represented the Palestinian point of view. In the end, I represent only myself and what I believe. Certainly, my commitment is not to neutrality or objectivity, in any event impossible to attain. Neutrality is often a mask

10

for siding with the *status quo*, while objectivity—pure objectivity at least—does not exist, and claiming it is dishonest. My commitment is to accuracy about both sides of the conflict, to representing the facts to each side about the other and to the world to the best of my ability. The commitment, fundamentally, is to be as close to knowledge as possible rather than to truth with a capital "T."

Committing oneself to a given issue forces one to confront the consciousness of what one really is and wishes to be. Who I am, what I represent, and the basis of my work[1] are deeply tied to my Holocaust

---

[1] This lecture is drawn from several of my recently published or soon to be published works. Rather than reference each section or paragraph (except where footnoted), I have chosen instead to cite all the works from which they are drawn: Sara Roy, "Preface—Humanism, Scholarship and Politics: Writing on the Palestinian-Israeli Conflict," *Failing Peace: Gaza and the Palestinian-Israeli Conflict* (London: Pluto Press, 2007), xi–xxiii; "Living with the Holocaust: The Journey of a Child of Holocaust Survivors," *Journal of Palestine Studies* 32.1 (Autumn 2002): 5–12 [Editor's Note: also available online at: www.bintjbeil.com/ E/occupation/roy_holocaust..htm (accessed 5/16/16)]; "A Jewish Plea," *The War on Lebanon: A Reader* (ed. Nubar Hovsepian; Northampton, MA: Olive Branch Press, 2008), 302–313 [Editor's note: also available online at: www.palestinechronicle.com/sara-roy-a-jewish-lea/?print =pdf (accessed 5/16/16)]; "Gaza: No se puede mirar—One cannot look"—A Brief Reflection," *Gaza as Metaphor* (ed. Helga Tawil-

background, which cannot help but transform how I look at the world. The concerns that propel me are rooted in the belief that there is an essential humanity in all people. As a child of Holocaust survivors I have, throughout my life, experienced, insofar as I was capable, the meaning of lives extinguished, futures taken, and histories silenced. Although my parents survived the horror and went on to live full and productive lives, they were never again who they once were. There was always within them a mournful longing for those they loved so much and lost, a longing that could never be resolved.

One of my greatest struggles, as a child of survivors, is how to remember those who perished. How do we speak of their lives—how do we celebrate those lives—beyond the carnage and destruction? How do we preserve and protect their identity as human beings while grieving for them? The themes of my life have always centered on the loss of humanity and its reclamation, and on its amazing resilience even in the face of unimaginable cruelty. That these themes

Souri and Dina Matar; London: Hurst, 2016); and "Introduction to the Third Edition: De-development Completed? Making Gaza Unviable," and "Afterword—The Wars on Gaza: A Reflection," *The Gaza Strip: The Political Economy of De-development* (3rd ed.; Washington, DC: Institute for Palestine Studies, 2015).

would extend to my work with Palestinians and Israelis was not random.

Many of the people—Jewish and otherwise—who write about Palestinians fail to accept the fundamental humanity of the people they are writing about, a failing based on ignorance, fear, and racism. Within the Jewish community especially, it has always been unacceptable to claim that Palestinians are like us, that they possess an essential humanity and must be included within our moral boundaries. As one Israeli friend of mine put it, "The one thing Israelis totally refuse [to do and] are incapable of doing, is placing themselves in the shoes of Palestinians." It has been unacceptable to claim that any attempt at separation is artificial, preferring distance to proximity.

Do we choose to be among "those who memorialize the dead in institutional and liturgical settings," asks the religious scholar Marc Ellis, "or [among] those who recognize and accompany the victims created in the shadow of the Holocaust?"[1] What is at stake in our continued (mis)representation of the other is the loss of our own humanity and our faith in a common humanity. Such willful blindness can

---

[1] See Marc H. Ellis, *Practicing Exile* (Minneapolis: Fortress, 2002), 59.*

cause the destruction of principle and a "careless indifference to grand causes [that] has its counterpart in abdication in the face of force," to quote the French philosopher Alain Finkielkraut.[1] Indeed, the difference between maintaining our humanity and abandoning it is often slight and lies in remaining faithful to our ethics rather than to our tribe.

By reflecting on who we are and what we stand for, we are also engaged in a process of self-investigation, of judging and understanding our own behavior from viewpoints not our own. If real detachment is possible and has a role, it is in enabling us to see ourselves as others see us, using what Doris Lessing called the "other eye."[2] And a critical component of this lies in maintaining a living connection with the people whose problems we are trying to understand, experiencing with them the

---

[1] Alain Finkielkraut, "A Pair of Boots is as Good as Shakespeare," *Education in France: Continuity and Change in the Mitterand Years 1981–95* (ed. Anne Corbert and Bob Moon; New York: Routledge, 2004), 327–34, 347–48, here 348 n.15. Also see Roger Kimball, "The Treason of the Intellectuals & 'The Undoing of Thought,'" *The New Criterion* 34.9 (December 1992). Available online at: https://www.newcriterion.com/ articles.cfm/The-treason-of-the-intellectuals----ldquo-The-Undoing-of-Thought-rdquo--4648 (accessed 5/13/16).*

[2] See especially, Doris Lessing, *Prisons We Choose to Live Inside* (Milton, PA: Flamingo Press, 1993).*

conditions of their lives, accounting for "the experience of subordination itself," making those connections, Said says, that allow us to "unearth the forgotten" and create linkages too often denied— helping us learn "what to connect with, how, and how not."[1]

At the core of this needed connection, writes Jacqueline Rose, lies a "plea for peoples, however much history has turned them into enemies, to enter into each other's predicaments, to make what... [is] one of the hardest journeys of the mind."[2] Here I would like to quote from the Israeli filmmaker Shira Geffen, who tells about her visit six years ago to the West Bank home of the first female Palestinian suicide bomber, Wafa Idris:

> I was scared. It was my first time in Ramallah, and before I entered her home, I was really afraid of what I would say, how I would speak with her mother. I had a lot of fears. And then, when I went in, I saw an elderly, tired woman, and the first thing she did when she saw me was hug me. I saw behind her a huge poster of her dead daughter, and during this hug I suddenly

---

[1] See Edward Said, *Representations of the Intellectual: The 1993 Reith Lectures* (New York: Vintage, 1996), esp. 16–18.*

[2] Jacqueline Rose, Suffering and Injustice Enough for Everyone—On Empathy and the Complexity of Political Life: Essay in Honor of Edward Said, Draft, May 2004.*

felt her daughter, the one she didn't have. It was all mixed in my head. I was suddenly her daughter, who wanted to kill me, and this confusion—the understanding that all is one, and suffering is suffering, and that a woman who loses her daughter is a woman who loses her daughter no matter where, and that I can be anyone's daughter...[1]

Humanizing the other, who is often perceived as the enemy, is, in my view, a critical task of the writer, the humanist scholar, the activist. For it is only with such understanding of the other—especially, perhaps, a shared understanding of suffering and loss—that will allow us to find and then embrace what joins us and not what separates us. In order to do so, however, one must hold to a universal and single standard of basic human justice (and of seeking knowledge), despite ethnic or national affiliation. It cannot be otherwise.

If it is wrong to harm Israelis, then it is just as wrong to harm Palestinians, Rwandans, Yemenis, or Americans. Anything short of this requires a kind of ethical and intellectual contortion and inconsistency that has no place in humanistic endeavor. A lesson I

---

[1] Nirit Anderman, "Israeli Artist Shira Geffen Takes the Heat for Criticizing the War in Gaza," *HaAretz* (April 27, 2015). Available online at: http://www.haaretz.com/israel-news/culture/television/.premium-1.653671 (accessed 6/30/16).*

learned from a very young age from my mother and father was that justice applied selectively is no longer justice but discrimination. Moral ambivalence is not moral and becomes, inevitably, repression. The task, ultimately, of the humanist scholar is to universalize crisis, to give greater human scope to suffering, and "to [link] that experience with the sufferings of others."[1]

Yet, this is seldom the case. To the contrary, we fight hard for our known beliefs, refusing to change the pattern of our understanding and lacking the courage to confront a history that demands to be retold. Embedded in this struggle is a choice, a very difficult choice between inclusion and exclusion and their attendant consequences.

On Dissent

Why is it so difficult, even impossible, to accommodate Palestinians in the Jewish understanding of history? Why is there so little perceived need to question our own history and the one we have given others, preferring instead to embrace beliefs and sentiments that remain unchanged?

---

[1] Edward W. Said, *Representations of the Intellectual*, 44.*

17

Why is it virtually mandatory among Jewish intellectuals to oppose racism, repression, and injustice almost anywhere in the world, but unacceptable—indeed, for some heretical—to oppose it when Israel is the oppressor? For many among us, history and memory appear to preclude reflection and tolerance, where, says the literary critic Northrop Frye, "the enemy becomes not people to be defeated, but embodiments of an idea to be exterminated."[1] "No," wrote Doris Lessing, "I cannot imagine any nation—or not for long—teaching its citizens to become individuals able to resist group pressures."[2]

Yet, there are always individuals who do. Within the Jewish tradition (but by no means exclusive to it), dissent and argument are old and revered values. They are deeply embedded in Jewish life, be it religious or secular, political or Talmudist, but as in any tradition, they are less valued (and at times vilified) when the dissenter stands against his own group, against what Hannah Arendt called their organic sense of history.[3]

---

[1] Northrop Frye, "The Knowledge of Good and Evil," *The Morality of Scholarship* (Max Black, ed.; Ithaca: Cornell University Press, 1967), 9.*

[2] Doris Lessing, *Prisons We Choose to Live Inside*, 62.*

[3] See, for example, Hannah Arendt, *The Origins of Totalitarianism* (New York: Harcourt, Brace, Jovanovich, 1973).*

James Baldwin similarly asks, how does one stand apart from the "habits of thought [that] reinforce and sustain the habits of power"? In essence, how does an individual come into his or her humanity?[1]

For me, being an outsider from within means speaking with an unclaimed voice, beyond what we as a people have been given and educated to see, but very much from within our own tradition. Being a part of the Jewish community does not mean accepting (often uncritically) the social laws that govern us, the self-perception of our members, or the collective "we." It does mean situating oneself within a cultural value system and choosing ethical consistency over collective engagement, exposure over concealment. It means insisting on the legitimacy of criticism of unjust policies; without such criticism, to quote Lear, "lies madness."[2]

In one of his last works, Edward Said wrote that the "intellectual is perhaps a kind of counter-memory, with its own counter-discourse that will not allow

---

[1] See JoAnn Wypijewski, "James Baldwin: A Guide in Dark Times," *The Nation* (January 21, 2015). Available online at: www.thenation.com/article/james-baldwin-guide-dark-times/ (accessed 6/29/16).*

[2] William Shakespeare, *King Lear* (ed. Joseph Pearce; Ignatius Critical Editions; San Francisco: Ignatius Press, 2008), 3.4.21.*

conscience to look away or fall asleep. The best corrective… is to imagine the person whom you are discussing—in this case the person on whom the bombs will fall—reading you in your presence."[1]

Yet those who challenge the assumptions held so sacred by their group are often disqualified as marginal and traitorous, existing outside the bounds of legitimacy and influence—although I must say this has been changing.

Speaking from beyond the Sacred
The Holocaust and Judaism, Israel and Gaza

The Holocaust has been the defining feature of my life. It could not have been otherwise. I lost over 100 members of my family in the Nazi ghettos and death camps in Poland—grandparents, aunts, uncles, cousins, a sibling not yet born—people from the shtetls of Poland whom I never knew, but who have always been part of my life.

Although I cannot be certain, I think my first real encounter with the Holocaust was when I first noticed the number the Nazis had imprinted on my father's arm. To his oppressors, my father, Abraham,

---

[1] Edward Said, *Humanism and Democratic Criticism* (New York: Columbia University Press, 2004), 142–43.*

had no name, no history, and no identity other than that blue-inked number. As a small child of four or five, I remember asking my father why he had that number on his arm. He answered that he had once painted it on, but then found that it would not wash off, so was left with it.

My father was one of six children, and he was the only one in his family to survive the Holocaust. He was one of seven known survivors of the first Nazi extermination camp in Chelmno, Poland, where 150,000 Jews were murdered, including the majority of my family on both my father's and mother's sides. Abraham was the first person ever to escape a Nazi death camp. He also survived Auschwitz. I know little about my father's family because he could not speak about them without breaking down. It caused me such pain to see him suffer with his memories that I stopped asking him to share them.

My mother, Taube, was one of nine children—seven girls and two boys. Her father, Herschel, was a rabbi and *shohet*—a ritual slaughterer—and deeply loved and respected by all who knew him. Herschel was a learned man who had studied with some of the great rabbis of Poland. As a family they lived very modestly, but every Sabbath my grandfather would bring home a poor or homeless person who was seated at the head of the table to share the Sabbath meal.

My mother and her sister Frania were the only two in their family to survive the war, except for another sister, Shoshana, who had immigrated to Palestine in 1936. My mother and aunt Frania had managed never to be separated throughout the entire war—through seven years in the Pabanice and Lodz ghettos, followed by the Auschwitz and Halbstadt concentration camps—except for one time at Auschwitz. They were in a selection line, where Jews were lined up and their fate sealed by the Nazi doctor Josef Mengele, who determined who would live and who would die. When my aunt came before him, he sent her to the right, to labor (a temporary reprieve). When my mother approached him, he sent her to the left, to death, which meant she would be gassed. Miraculously, my mother managed to sneak back into the selection line, and when she approached Mengele again, he sent her to labor.

After the war ended, my aunt Frania desperately wanted to go to Palestine to join Shoshana, who had been there for ten years. The creation of a Jewish state was imminent, and Frania felt it was the only safe place for Jews after the Holocaust. My mother disagreed and refused to go. She often spoke

22

to me of that decision, explaining that her refusal to live in Israel was based on her belief, learned and reinforced by her experiences during the war, that tolerance, compassion, and justice cannot be practiced nor extended when one lives only among one's own. "I could not live as a Jew among Jews alone," she would tell me. "For me, it wasn't possible. I wanted to live as a Jew in a pluralist society, where my group remained important to me, but where others were important to me, too."

I grew up in a home where Judaism was defined and practiced not as a religion but as a system of ethics and culture. My first language was Yiddish. My home was filled with joy and optimism, though punctuated at times by grief and loss. The notion of a Jewish homeland was important to my parents, but unlike many of their friends, they were not uncritical of Israel. Obedience to a state was not an ultimate Jewish value for them. Judaism provided the context for Jewish life, for values and beliefs that transcended national boundaries. For my mother and father, Judaism meant bearing witness, raging against injustice, and foregoing silence. It meant compassion, tolerance, and rescue. It meant always hearing the voice of the victim no matter who he or she was. It meant, as Ammiel Alcalay has written, ensuring to the extent possible that the memories of the past do not become the memories of the future.[1] In the absence of these imperatives, they taught me, we cease to be Jews.

The Holocaust is not a shield beyond which you cannot look, my mother and father insisted; rather, it is a mirror with which to reflect and examine your actions, a mirror you must always carry with you. In this regard, the Holocaust was always presented to me in terms that were both particular (i.e., Jewish) and universal, and the two, they believed, were indivisible. To separate them would diminish the meaning of both.

Despite many visits to Israel during my youth, the first time I visited the occupied territories was in the summer of 1985, two and a half years before the first Palestinian uprising. I was conducting fieldwork for my doctoral dissertation, which examined American economic assistance to the West Bank and Gaza Strip and whether or not it was possible to promote economic development under conditions of military occupation. That summer changed my life because it was then that I came to experience the Israeli occupation for the first time. I learned how it works, its

---

[1] See Ammiel Alcalay, *Memories of Our Future: Selected Essays 1982–1999* (Los Angeles: Skylights Press, 2001).*

24

effects on the economy, on daily life, its grinding impact on people. I learned what it meant to have little control over one's life and, more importantly, over the lives of one's children.

As with the Holocaust, I tried to remember my first real encounter with the occupation. One of the earliest was a scene I witnessed standing on a street with some Palestinian friends. An elderly man was walking along leading his donkey. A small child of no more than three or four, clearly his grandson, was with him. All of a sudden some nearby Israeli soldiers approached the old man and stopped him. One of them went over to the donkey and pried open its mouth. "Old man," he asked, "why are your donkey's teeth so yellow? Don't you brush your donkey's teeth?" The old Palestinian was mortified, the little boy visibly upset.

The soldier repeated his question, yelling this time, while the other soldiers laughed. The child began to cry and the old man just stood there silently, humiliated. As the scene continued a crowd gathered. The soldier then ordered the old man to stand behind the donkey and demanded that he kiss the animal's behind. At first, the old man refused but as the soldier screamed at him and his grandson became hysterical, he bent down and did it. The soldiers laughed and walked away. We all stood there in silence, ashamed to look at each other, the only sound the sobs of the little boy. The old man, demeaned and destroyed, did not move for what seemed a very long time.

I stood in stunned disbelief. I immediately thought of the stories my parents had told me of how Jews had been treated by the Nazis in the 1930s, before the ghettos and death camps, of how Jews would be forced to clean sidewalks with toothbrushes and have their beards cut off in public. What happened to the Palestinian grandfather was equivalent in principle, intent, and impact: to humiliate and dehumanize. In this critical respect, my first encounter with the occupation was the same as my first encounter with the Holocaust, with the number on my father's arm. It spoke the same message: the denial of one's humanity.

Is It Wrong to Compare?

I have long been warned about making any kind of comparison or drawing any kind of parallel between the Jewish victims of the Holocaust and the Palestinians living under Israeli occupation. Some friends have told me, some screaming at me, that I weaken my argument with such parallels and de-legitimize myself. More importantly, they say, I defile the memory of the six million—among whom are my grandparents, aunts, and uncles—by invoking their names alongside Palestinian ones.

Yet, however vast the difference in scope, however lacking in symmetry and equivalence the experiences, the Holocaust and the Palestinian issues in a sense *are* related. Among the many realities that frame contemporary Jewish life are the birth of Israel, remembrance of the Holocaust, and Jewish power and sovereignty. And it cannot be denied that the latter has a critical corollary: the displacement and oppression of the Palestinian people. For Jewish identity is linked, willingly or not, to Palestinian suffering and this suffering is now an irrevocable part of our collective memory and an intimate part of our experience, together with the Holocaust and Israel. This is a linkage that informs the core of Ellis's work.[1] How, he asks, are we to celebrate our Jewishness while others are being oppressed? Is the Jewish covenant with God present or absent in the face of Jewish oppression of Palestinians? Is the Jewish ethical tradition still available to us? Is the promise of holiness—so central to Jewish existence—

---

[1] For more on Roy's assessment of the work of Marc Ellis, see Sara Roy, *Failing Peace*, 25–29.*

27

now beyond our ability to reclaim? For the answers, at least in part, I look to Gaza.

Where Civilians Do Not Exist

Today, Gaza finds itself in an unknown and precarious place, deprived of the ordinary and comprehensible. After nearly fifty years of occupation, twenty-four years of closure, nine years of blockade, and three wars waged against them in six years, Palestinians in Gaza see no horizon or future beyond the panorama of destruction that now confronts them, a reality without precedent. According to the UN, 2014 was the deadliest year for Palestinians since 1967, given the horrendous losses inflicted by Operation Protective Edge in the summer of 2014.[1] Over my three decades of involvement with Gaza, I have witnessed the deliberate and purposeful disablement of this vibrant place and its gentle people—and now its large-scale destruction, and I continue to ask myself, why?

In her book *The Body in Pain*, Elaine Scarry shows that "torture in its essence is a discourse, a teaching, what is being taught is the futility of acting like a subject, of aspiring to anything beyond abject

---

[1] See www.ohchr.org/EN/HRBodies/HRC/ColGaza Conflict/ Pages/ReportColGaza.aspx (accessed 5/16/16).*

survival."[1] Gazans continue to struggle against such debasement; yet of all the miseries that they have endured, one continues to preoccupy them more than all the others—an entreaty that still remains unheard: the unconstrained battle for human dignity.

This battle is constant and unrelenting, as ferocious in its insistency as are the attempts by Israel to extinguish it. There is a voice that has always been present through all my years of research among Palestinians and it speaks these words: we, too, are mothers and fathers, sisters and brothers, professors and lawyers, fishermen and factory workers. We, too, are human beings with individual histories and stories that must be recounted by the living, not only buried with the dead.

Gaza is a place, Israel argues, where innocent civilians do not exist. The presence of such civilians in

---

[1] Paul Aaron, "Witness to War: Assessing the Impact on Life in Gaza," Presentation on a panel entitled, *Abandoned Yet Central: Gaza and the Resolution of the Israeli-Palestinian Conflict*, Middle East Studies Association Meeting, November 23, 2014, Washington, DC. Original source: Lawrence Weschler, *A Miracle, A Universe: Settling Scores with Torturers* (Chicago: University of Chicago Press, 1990), 237. [Ed. Note: Similarly, see Lawrence Weschler, "A Miracle, a Universe: Settling Accounts with Torturers," *Transitional Justice: How Emerging Democracies Reckon with Former Regimes* (ed. Neil J. Kritz; Washington, DC: United States Institute of Peace, 1995), 1: 491–99, here 492.]

Gaza is suspect, they say, because Palestinians elected a terrorist organization to represent them. Retired Israeli Major General Giora Eiland stated, "[T]hey [Gazans] are to blame for this situation just like Germany's residents were to blame for electing Hitler as their leader and paid a heavy price for that, and rightfully so."[1] The goal is to use "disproportionate force," said another official, thereby "inflicting damage and meting out punishment to an extent that will demand long and expensive reconstruction processes."[2] According to this logic there is no such thing as a civilian home, school, hospital, mosque, church, or playground in Gaza; all these places are therefore legitimate targets of Israeli bombs since every home is a non-home; every kindergarten a non-kindergarten; and every hospital a non-hospital.

During Operation Cast Lead (OCL), Israel's 2008–09 offensive against Gaza, Reserve Major Amiran Levin similarly stated, "What we have to do is act

---

[1] Giora Eiland, "In Gaza, There Is No Such Thing as 'Innocent Civilians,'" *YNet News.com* (May 8, 2014). Available online at: http://www.ynetnews.com/articles/0,7340,L-4554583,00.html (accessed 6/29/16).*

[2] Col. (Ret.) Gabriel Siboni, quoted in *The Goldstone Report: The Legacy of the Landmark Investigation of the Gaza Conflict* (ed. Adam Horowitz, Lizzy Ratner and Philip Weiss; New York: Nations Books, 2011), 191.*

systematically with the aim of punishing all the organizations that are firing the rockets and mortars as well as the civilians who are enabling them to fire and hide," while the IDF spokesperson Major Avital Leibowitz argued that "anything affiliated with Hamas is a legitimate target." Not surprisingly the UN-commissioned Goldstone Report whose mandate it was to investigate all violations of international human rights and humanitarian law that might have been committed during OCL found that the "humiliation and dehumanization of the Palestinian population" were Israeli policy objectives in its assault on Gaza, an assault that was nothing less than "a deliberately disproportionate attack designed to punish, humiliate and terrorize a civilian population, radically diminish its local economic capacity both to work and to provide for itself, and to force upon it an ever increasing sense of dependency and vulnerability."[1]

That the area being bombed was urban, with over 20,000 human beings per square kilometer, does

---

[1] See Sara Roy, *Hamas and Civil Society in Gaza: Engaging the Islamist Social Sector* (Princeton Studies in Muslim Politics; Princeton: Princeton University Press, 2013), 235, 318 n.49. The Goldstone Report is available online at: www2.ohchr.org/english/bodies/hrcouncil/docs/12session/A-HRC-12-48.pdf (accessed 5/16/16).*

not weigh on the majority of Jewish people. That my friends and their children were among those being bombed, people who have always welcomed me as a Jew into their homes in Gaza, is of no consequence. "22 members of my family huddled under the stairwell," describes Hani, who lived in the heart of Shejaiyeh, one of the areas that witnessed the greatest destruction that summer.

> Parents, sisters, brothers, aunts, uncles. We stayed there until 10 the next morning when there was a lull, which is when we were able to escape. During the night, I tried to keep track of the number of explosions. I stopped counting at 866. Every thirty seconds there was shell or a bomb. The walls of the buildings were sheared off but they fell out rather than in. My sister said we are all going to die. She went to each of us and kissed us, told us how much she loved us and said goodbye.[1]

For General Eiland, Majors Levin and Leibowitz, and too many others, there are no parents in Gaza, there are no children or sisters or brothers; there are no deaths to mourn. Rather, Gaza is where the grass grows wild and must be mowed from time to time. The desolation inflicted on Gaza is powerfully seen in the

---

[1] Paul Aaron, "Witness to War: Assessing the Impact on Life in Gaza."*

almost complete destruction of Khuza'a, a village once known as Gaza's orchard. Writes a UN colleague soon after the ceasefire that ended Operation Protective Edge:

> Khuza'a was very difficult. There are whole stretches with every dwelling smashed, and untouched land between them. People are living in two- and three-walled rooms. There is almost no sign of the neighborhood economy until you drive some blocks back—but also no sign of transport for people to reach the trading. We saw only one little micro-enterprise cart of the kind that normally fills neighborhoods. It feels as though they are miles away from any kind of community, and I can't begin to imagine the impact of staring at jagged wreckage day after day. When they see the big UN car, everyone drifts toward it, sometimes hailing it and sometimes angry or just desperate to tell someone what they are living through.

What had been a lively neighborhood has been reduced, so suddenly, to complete dependence. They fell through the floor of any kind of humane standard... there is a fragility in these areas that I find frightening.

The devastation of Khuza'a (and Beit Hanun, Shejaiya, Beit Lahiya) conceals an even greater theft that has long been imposed on Palestinians, especially in Gaza: the desecration of daily life. Professor Nadera Shalhoub-Kevorkian writes that Palestinians live in "a zone of non-existence" where one finds "new spaces of obscenity in the politics of day-to-day lives."[1] These obscene spaces are defined by a maimed reality where engaging in normal, everyday acts of living and working—building a home, going to school, visiting relatives, planting a tree, playing in a park, or sitting on a beach—are treated as criminal activities, punishable even by death.

This begs the question, can Jews as a people be ordinary, an essential part of our rebirth after the Holocaust? Is it possible to be normal when we seek remedy and comfort in the dispossession and destruction of another people, "[o]bserving the windows of [their] houses through the sites of rifles," to borrow from the Israeli poet, Almog Behar?[2]

How can we create when we consent so willingly and with such complacence to the demolition of homes, construction of barriers, denial of sustenance, and ruin of innocents? How can we be merciful when speaking out against the wanton

---

[1] See Sara Roy, "2012 Edward Said Memorial Lecture," *The Jerusalem Fund*, Transcript No. 374 (10 October 2012). Available online at: www.thejerusalemfund.org/4373/2012-edward-said-memorial-lecture (accessed 6/29/16).*

[2] See www.almogbehar.wordpress.com/english/ (accessed 6/29/16).*

murder of children, of whole families and of entire neighborhoods is considered an act of disloyalty and betrayal rather than a legitimate act of dissent, and where dissent is so ineffective and reviled? How can we be humane when, to use Jacqueline Rose's words, we seek "omnipotence as the answer to historical pain?"[1]

Instead we condone the cruelty, even celebrating the murder of Palestinians while remaining the abused, "creating situations where our victimization is assured and our innocence affirmed" as seen in the words of General Eiland: "Because we want to be compassionate towards those cruel people [in Gaza], we are committing to act cruelly towards the really compassionate people – the residents of the State of Israel."[2] In this way, Gaza speaks to the unnaturalness of our own condition as Jews.

Will we one day be able to live without the walls we are constantly asked to build? When will we be obliged to acknowledge our limits?

---

[1] Jacqueline Rose, *The Last Resistance* (New York: Verso, 2007), 155–56.*

[2] Eiland, "In Gaza, There Is No Such Thing as 'Innocent Civilians.'"*

Gaza, Israel, and the End of Holocaust Consciousness

One of the most powerful works of Holocaust literature I have read is Yehiel De-Nur's *Shivitti: A Vision*. He signed this book, as he did his others, not with his name but with the number he was given in Auschwitz: Ka-Tzetnik 135633 (KZ being the initials of "concentration camp" in German and pronounced "ka-tzet"). He did so in memory of every camp inmate who was known by "Ka-Tzetnik Number...," the number itself branded into the flesh of the left arm[1] as was my father's.

In what is perhaps the most memorable passage of the book, De-Nur describes how he hid in a coal bin inside a crematorium truck, which was parked and locked in a garage. Reliving the moment when he escaped from the truck, De-Nur, covered in coal dust, encounters a stunned garage superintendent who is an SS officer, and screams at him, "I'm a human being. No evil spirit! No demon! I am human and I want to live! I am a human being! Human!"—the same words I hear cried in Gaza, words meant to affirm existence and self-worth.[2]

---

[1] Ka-Tzetnik 135633, *Shivitti: A Vision* (San Francisco: Harper & Row, 1989), jacket.

[2] See Ka-Tzetnik 135633, *Shivitti*, 106.*

During Israel's 2014 assault, Raji Sourani, a prominent human rights lawyer in Gaza, wrote me:

> Gaza is a totally unsafe place. Day and night the same: shock and terror... Airplanes do not leave Gaza's skies and they are throwing death to children and women. I visited the intensive care unit at Shifa Hospital and you cannot imagine the scene; most of them will die soon. Even medicines do not exist—almost 40 percent shortages. The hospital is full of women and children; many lost [body] parts and limbs... People here have nothing to lose except misery and humiliation... We want to live a normal life, with dignity.

He also told me: "We will not be good victims."

Another friend, Sami Abdel-Shafi, a political analyst and the Gaza representative of the Atlanta-based Carter Center, sent me the following during some of the worst days of the bombing: "Gaza is being slaughtered. Innocents who are in favor of peace are being slaughtered... My God. My God, the God of all good people."

In another distressing email to me, Sami recounted the following:

> I am barely sleeping from utter worry and fear, a new kind I haven't had [since] 2008/09. Stories of civilian targeting on the streets and at home are [terrifying]. Unbelievable. So often, I spend my time running from one place to the

other around the house fearing what may come. I started mistaking the sound of boiling water on the stove as though it is something descending from the sky... You don't know when it will start, where, for what reason or how long it will [last]. Sheer paranoia.

As I pictured Sami running from one room to another trying desperately to find a place of safety, a family story from the Holocaust immediately pressed its way into my memory, a story I try hard not to recall because of the pain it always inflicts. The Nazis came to the *shtetl* where my grandparents lived. All of their nine children—my mother, aunts, and uncles—were adults and no longer lived at home except for my aunt Frania (who told me this story) and my aunt Sophie who was only 12 years old. Before emptying the town of its Jewish inhabitants, the Nazis decided to take their children first. On the day they came for Sophie, my grandfather and grandmother frantically ran through the rooms of their home searching for a place—a closet, a chest, a cupboard—to hide Sophie from the destruction that ultimately claimed her. My grandparents succeeded at first but eventually she was taken—as they were—and never seen again.

How can I not think of those innocents murdered in Gaza last summer—among them 548 children—alongside my grandfather, grandmother, and Sophie? Refusing any such association or bond, as I have been told I must do, is not only the end of Holocaust consciousness, it is the end of Jewish ethical history—shattering the mirror I promised my parents always to use.

We Must Rise from the Ashes but Can We?

There are among Israelis real feelings of vulnerability and fear, never resolved but exploited and intensified. Israel is the occupier yet the fear remains. What kind of future do we as a people face?

My children's generation will be the first without any living witness to the Holocaust. As Avrum Burg, the former Speaker of the Israeli Parliament has said, "That will be the generation in which... personal experience becomes a memory. What will be the shape of that memory?" he asks. A cloning of the trauma or a beginning of the road from trauma to trust?"[1] But how is that trust to be created?

Judaism has always prided itself on reflection, critical examination, and philosophical inquiry. The

---

[1] "Former Speaker of the Israeli Parliament Avraham Burg: 'The Holocaust is Over: We Must Rise from its Ashes,'" *Democracy Now*, Transcript (February 12, 2009). Available online at: www.democracynow.org/2009/2/12/former_speaker_of_ the _ israeli_parliament (accessed 7/29/16).*

Talmudic mind examines a sentence, a word, in a multitude of ways, seeking all possible interpretations and searching constantly for the one left unsaid. Through such scrutiny, it is believed, comes the awareness needed to protect the innocent, prevent injury or harm, and be closer to God.

Now such scrutiny is rejected, removed from our ethical system. Rather the imperative is to see through eyes that are closed, unfettered by investigation, whereas Ellis says, renewal and injustice are silently joined. Today it is not the disappearance of our ethical system that we must confront but its rewriting into something disfigured and unrecognizable. The Holocaust stands not as a lesson or as mirror as my parents implored, but as an internal act of purification where tribal attachment (nurtured on fear) rather than ethical responsibility (aimed at inclusion and the common good) is demanded and used to define collective and political action.

Are these the boundaries of our renaissance 70 years after the liberation of Auschwitz?

A Concluding Thought

"Early Sunday morning on August 3rd 2014," wrote an American friend living in Gaza, "an Israeli F-16 dropped two one-thousand pound bombs on the main buildings of the Islamic University in Gaza. With modern facilities, excellent teachers, an administration that honors academic excellence and steers clear of politics, and 20,000 loyal students—more than half female—the university is among the very best in all of Palestine," he writes.

In 2010, Noam Chomsky, visiting to receive an honorary degree, lectured on linguistics to a packed house. Twelve hours after the airstrike, the pristine campus was thick with the stench of burning. Scattered across the parking lot were exam papers from a course in English literature. Students had been asked to analyze William Butler Yeats' poem, "The Second Coming."[1]

Memory in Judaism—like all memory—is dynamic, not static, embracing a multiplicity of voices and shunning the hegemony of one. But in the post-Holocaust world, Jewish memory has failed in one critical respect: it has excluded the reality of Palestinian suffering and Jewish culpability therein. As a people, we have been unable to link the creation of Israel with the displacement and oppression of the Palestinians. To the contrary, because Israel's identity

---

[1] Paul Aaron, "Witness to War: Assessing the Impact on Life in Gaza."*

is so closely bound to the Holocaust, "to find fault with the Jewish state," writes the late Tony Judt, "is to think ill of Jews; even to imagine an alternative configuration in the Middle East," he says, "is to indulge the moral equivalent of genocide."[1]

Brian Klug, a professor of Philosophy at Oxford University, states it thus: "The situation now of Jews in much of the world is dominated not by an *anti*-Jewish state but a *Jewish* state; not by policies and actions that are directed *against* Jewish interests but *in the name* of those interests; and not by a hostile power (Germany) that occupies the lands where Jews live but by a friendly power (Israel) that occupies territory where *others* live."[2]

How, then do we move forward toward resolution?

For me the answer lies, fundamentally, in a question and a choice. The question is this: Who are we as Jews and what are our responsibilities? And to this question, I would add another that my mother and

---

[1] Tony Judt, "Israel: The Alternative," *The New York Review of Books*, October 23, 2003.*

[2] Brian Klug, "Does Moral Opposition to 'Operation Protective Edge' Translate into Antisemitism?" *The Critique* (April 1, 2015). Available online at: www.thecritique.com/articles/ does-moral-opposition-to-operation-protective-edge-translate-into-antisemitism (accessed 8/1/16).*

father would most certainly have asked: How do we as a people look into the mirror and see reflected back Palestinian pain and loss? The choice: either we bind the "interests of Jews to those of humanity at large" or we continue to separate them, "insisting," as Judt wrote, "upon identifying a universal Jewishness with one small piece of territory."[1]

Francesca Klug, a visiting professor at the London School of Economics, writes in her recently published book, *A Magna Carta for Humanity: Homing in on Human Rights,* that the 1948 Universal Declaration of Human Rights placed humanity over citizenship, making states accountable for the horrors they inflicted for the first time in history. The Charter was drafted to address the lessons of the Holocaust. Yet, she writes:

> six decades on, the Israeli government refutes all criticisms that emanate from the same international legal standards that developed directly out of Jewish oppression. When Israeli human rights groups protest against the occupation of Palestinian lands, or the blockade of Gaza, they are frequently accused of

---

[1] Tony Judt, "Israel Must Unpick its Ethnic Myth," *Financial Times*, December 7, 2009, online at: www.ft.com/cms/s/0/7f8fafee-e366-11de-8d36-00144feab49a.html#axzz3pbpXKEAs (accessed 8/1/16).*

betrayal. Yet they are applying the same ethical framework, which arose from the darkest periods as "a common standard" for "all peoples and all nations.[1]

I shall end with the words of Irena Klepfisz, a writer and poet, whose father died in the Warsaw ghetto uprising after having gotten her and her mother to safety. She writes:

> I have concluded that one way to pay tribute to those we loved who struggled, resisted and died is to hold on to their vision and their fierce outrage at the destruction of the ordinary life of their people. It is this outrage we need to keep alive in our daily life and apply it to all situations, whether they involve Jews or non-Jews. It is this outrage we must use to fuel our actions and vision whenever we see any signs of the disruptions of common life: the hysteria of a mother grieving for the teenager who has been shot; a family stunned in front of a vandalized or demolished home; a family separated, displaced; arbitrary and unjust laws that demand the closing or opening of shops and schools; humiliation of a people whose culture is alien and deemed inferior; a people left homeless without citizenship; a people living under military rule. Because of our experience, we recognize these evils as obstacles to peace. At those moments of recognition, we

---

[1] Francesca Klug, "Speaking Out for Human Rights," *Jewish Quarterly* 61.3–4 (2014): 74.*

> remember the past, feel the outrage that inspired the Jews of the Warsaw Ghetto and allow it to guide us in present struggles.[1]

Thus, we must remember those who died—not only to memorialize their deaths but to honor their lives by affirming the ordinary life of people, both Palestinian and Jewish, creating as Edward Said once said, the possibility of dreaming a different dream.

---

[1] Irena Klepfisz, "Yom Hashoah, Yom Yerushalayim: A Meditation," *Dreams of an Insomniac: Jewish Feminist Essays, Speeches and Diatribes* (Portland, OR: Eighth Mountain Press, 1980).*

Beyond Interfaith Reconciliation
Kairos Theology and the Challenge to the Church

Mark Braverman

I come before you today as an American, fully aware of my responsibility as an American citizen for the crime that is being committed in Palestine. I also stand before you as a Jew, deeply connected to my tradition and to my people, who is horrified and heartbroken over what is being done in my name: for the suffering of my Palestinian sisters and brothers in Palestine and in exile, for the psychological and spiritual peril of my own people who have imprisoned themselves behind the wall they have built. Israel is on a course that is unsustainable, sinful, and suicidal. I stand before you in mourning for the institutional Jewish community throughout the world that is still blind, that will someday be on its knees in contrition for what we have done. I feel like that Palestinian Jew of 2000 years ago who wept over a Jerusalem that was on the course of self-destruction, because it had forgotten God. At the same time, I am deeply grateful for the faithful witness of Christians, working so hard, so persistently, in the face of opposition and the blindness and false prophecy of much of the church itself. I am inspired and hopeful because of the emergence of a global church movement, the kairos movement, inspired by the courageous witness of the South African church under Apartheid in the 1980s, and the Palestinian church following three decades later.[1]

Kairos is hard to define. It is one of those brilliant, hard nuggets of a word that seems to contain a universe, and continues to expand its essence in an unlimited fashion. Kairos is, like theology itself, a living thing, constantly unfolding and expanding and deepening. Like theology, it is only alive when it is doing its job—helping us understand what God expects of us in relationship to our fellow creatures and the natural environment that has been given to us. Like theology, it is only valid as long as it remains in conversation with history. Kairos is a response to a proper reading of the signs of the times. Kairos time is the time when, in American theologian Robert McAfee Brown's words, "Opportunity demands a response.

---

[1] See http://www.kairospalestine.ps/ (accessed 8/1/16).*

God offers us a new set of possibilities and we have to accept or decline."[1]

Kairos presents what a friend once described to me as a case of "insurmountable opportunity." Even when—and usually this is the case—the objective is clear but the road uncertain, full of hazards, uncharted, you must go. Even in the face of opposition and persecution, you must go. And here we must revisit, as I will suggest we must do continually, the experience of those who lived the original Kairos, as recounted in the Acts of the Apostles:

"We cannot but speak of what
we have seen and heard." (4:19–20)
"We must obey God
rather than any human authority." (5:29)

This is a moment of truth for the church! The concept of *status confessionis* speaks to this: in Robert McAfee Brown's phrasing,

> when the issues become so clear, and the stakes so high, that the privilege of amiable disagreement (which Christians have proven themselves to be so good at—the ability to occupy both sides of every controversial question) must be superseded by clear cut

---

[1] Robert McAfee Brown, *Kairos: Three Prophetic Challenges to the Church* (Grand Rapids: Eerdmans, 1990), 3.*

decisions, and the choice must move from both/and to either/or.[1]

Working with the churches on the issue of Palestine is a political organizing strategy. The churches are powerful, they have shown themselves to be in the cases of our own civil rights movement and the anti-Apartheid movement. The churches need to be in alliance with secular grassroots peace and human rights movement organizations and popular resistance movements and with other, non-Christian faith groups—but the church is the focus here and I'll make that case.

This church setting has become very familiar to me. Often after I have preached from the lectionary at a church on Sunday, I am asked by a curious churchgoer, "when did you convert to Christianity?" Although asked innocently, for a Jew, given the painful history of Christian-Jewish relations over the millennia, it's a freighted question. At first, my answer that I have not become a Christian seemed sufficient, although probably leaving the questioner confused. But it has caused me a great deal of thought about what it means for my Jewish identity that I am so delighted by and inspired by the ministry of that Galilean Jew who, to

---

[1] Brown, *Kairos*, 7.

my mind, represents the core of what I was taught Judaism is about. It's very clear to me that Jesus was the very best of Jews—then, and still now. So my answer to the question now, perhaps just as confusing to the questioner, but far more satisfactory to me, is: "I don't know really what that would mean, but I wish that things had gone differently in the first century so that I would not have to be answering that question today."

Being Jewish is my identity—can't change it any more than I can change my skin. I treasure my heritage and what we brought to the world. But I believe that the divergence between the Jewish tradition and the faith community that came to be called Christianity, a divergence that has been called a fateful, one might say tragic, parting, was not about an argument about whether Jesus of Nazareth—the Palestinian Jew—was the foretold Messiah, or even if that is what the Jewish scriptures were saying in the texts that are quoted in that regard, but rather about disagreement on the core issue that absorbs the world even today—universality versus particularism: Is it us and them?

This is the question that Jesus addresses in the parable of the Good Samaritan (Luke 10:25–37). Who is my neighbor? It is the question of the woman at the well (John 4:1–42). Why are you talking to me? We worship on this mountain. You worship on that one. Remember what Jesus says to her. He says, the day is coming when we will worship God neither here nor there but in the spirit. Think of what he was saying. It is the core of the Christian message. It is what Jesus was saying, carrying out the campaign promise that he made in that first stump speech in Nazareth on that Sabbath. He opened up the scroll of Isaiah and read about releasing the captives and giving sight to the blind. He fulfilled that campaign promise when he entered Jerusalem on that last Sunday, Palm Sunday. Standing in front of the temple he said, "Destroy this temple." We'll come back to this story. It was a very political statement. It is the question Jesus answered on Pentecost. He was crucified. He was raised. The tomb was empty. He had made a couple of appearances to his disciples. He instructed them to go to Jerusalem and they would get power from the Holy Spirit. Remember what the disciples said to him? They said, Lord, are you going to bring the kingdom back to Israel? (Acts 1:6–11) They were talking about a king, an army, a temple, sovereignty, hegemony, the Jews in charge. And Jesus just said, "Whatever. Go to Jerusalem and wait." Then what happened? The power of the spirit came to them, not as a gentle voice, but as tongues of fire that knocked them to the ground. Total transformation was coming. They stood up and the power that had been given to them was that they were speaking in all the languages of the world, including Arabic. If you take a look in the second chapter of Acts, the list is a catalogue of all the languages of the known world (i.e., the Mediterranean basin). This is not rocket science. What Pentecost is about, what is called the birth of the church, is that the good news is for everyone. This is the new law. This is what Torah means.

I once asked my friend Brian McLaren, a gifted evangelical pastor and writer, whether I was offending Christian colleagues in talking about Jesus as a prophet. To Christians, after all, Jesus may have been a prophet, but he was more than that. Brian responded that he was less concerned if people consider Jesus to be *more* than a prophet than he was that we see Jesus as *less than a prophet.* In other words, that we take care to honor how much Jesus stood in the prophetic tradition, a tradition in which one is enjoined to speak truth to power, to actively oppose systems that in their greed and hunger for power betray the most fundamental values of both traditions to care for the earth and for our fellow creatures, especially the most vulnerable. Indeed Jesus did this consistently, challenging the powers and principalities of his time, the establishment of king and priest installed in Jerusalem. Jesus was not challenging Rome. He was challenging the client government that worked for Rome. The temple (i.e., church of his time) was merged with political power to impoverish their own people to feed the beast of Empire. This is the message that brings us together here at this conference, whether or not we identify with a religious tradition or community—united in that we all face the same fundamental issues of racism and inequality, of exclusion versus inclusion in our cities, our nations, and even our faith communities, urgent issues that we must confront directly or face the catastrophic consequences.

These are the values that informed my upbringing as a Jew—principles of equality, human dignity, and compassion that are fundamental to the civil code of Torah and the words and actions of the Old Testament prophets as they spoke truth to power, values intertwined with the rich heritage I inherited and the beautiful rituals and holidays of the Jewish liturgical year. I love these traditions. I am steeped in it, but a cloud hung over my Jewish upbringing. If you are a Jewish kid like me, born into a traditional Jewish family, in a strong Jewish community, after World War II, after the establishment of the State of Israel, closely related to the history of Jewish suffering, then you were raised in a very potent combination of rabbinic Judaism and political Zionism. The two are not separate. It is in our liturgy. There is a prayer that was developed by the chief rabbi of Israel in 1948. We say it every day. "May God bless and protect the State of Israel." Bless the State of Israel—not Zion, not Jerusalem, but the State of Israel. In many synagogues the flag is there. The State of Israel is the first flowering of our redemption. It is theological.

Don't let anyone tell you that Zionism is a secular movement. Maybe it is atheistic, but it is also Messianic. David Ben Gurion was a messianic, fanatic genius. He thought that traditional Orthodox Judaism would wither away with the birth of the State of Israel. The opposite has happened. The State of Israel represents rich, fertile soil for fundamentalist Judaism. So, we have been redeemed from two thousand years of suffering and marginalization and I am blessed to have been born at that time. One small miracle is that they didn't name me "Israel." And I embraced this exceptionalist, privileged, eternally innocent narrative until I witnessed the occupation of Palestine in 2006. When I saw the dispossession and oppression that was being perpetrated in my name, it broke my heart. It tore me apart. It challenged all of my assumptions and beliefs. Then I learned another narrative—the *Nakba* (i.e., the Arabic word for "catastrophe"). Most importantly, I met the Palestinians. I recognized them and embraced them as my sisters and brothers as they did me and I realized that if my own people—the Jews—were going to survive, we would have to transcend our sense of specialness. I call it *victim-tinged entitlement*. Marc Ellis calls it eternal "innocence."[1] This sense was incubated for over two thousand years and has now taken the form of political Zionism—the claim that the land is ours by birthright and inheritance.

As a Jew born into a traditional Jewish family in 1948, three years after the fall of Nazi Germany and a month before the establishment of the State of Israel, I was raised in combination of rabbinic Judaism and political Zionism. I was taught that a miracle had blessed my generation. The State of Israel was redemption from two thousand years of suffering and slaughter. We had been redeemed. The suffering and the helplessness were over. I embraced this narrative.

---

[1] See Marc H. Ellis, *Israel and Palestine—Out of the Ashes: The Search for Jewish Identity in the Twenty-First Century* (London: Pluto Press, 2001).*

In no small measure thanks to the love and guidance from Palestinian sisters and brothers, as well as some courageous Jewish voices in Israel and in the United States, I have been liberated from Zionism and in the process have claimed my true Jewishness—the Jewishness I've been looking for all my life. With it came my identification with that very good Jew from Nazareth, who was born into imperial occupation, a condition of absolute evil that propelled and shaped his ministry, a Jew who called his own people, and, pointedly, their leadership of king and priests, back to God, back to Torah. The parallels between the first century and the twenty-first century are so striking to me. One of the things that we need to do is to make sure that when people make their devotional pilgrimages and tourist trips to Jerusalem that they see what needs to be seen. I think we need a sort of brochure that says, "Walk where Jesus walked, but see what Jesus saw." What Jesus saw was Imperial oppression—a people trampled under military oppression that was trying to dispossess them and take away their rights. Of course, the Romans did not exile the Jews.[1] That they did is part of the historical myth.

---

[1] See, for example, Jerry Haber, "No, Rivkele, The Jews Weren't Driven into Exile by the Romans," *The Magnes Zionist*

And neither did the British nor the Ottomans nor any of the other rulers of Palestine. Only Israel is involved in ethnic cleansing (i.e., dispossession and banishment).

So, as a Jew today, I have to talk about Palestine. Contemplating twenty-first century Palestine, which bears such startling resemblance to Palestine of the first century, I must recognize and declare that my story is not about my past suffering or the crimes committed against my people, but rather it is about the suffering we are causing today, the crimes of which we are guilty. The problem is not Holocaust denial or even Holocaust obsession. The problem is that we are blocked from seeing the Jewish story of today (i.e., not the story of Jewish suffering), but the story of suffering we are causing others. Then, if there is any way to make meaning of the Holocaust, it is to embrace the Palestinian cause and the cause of all people who suffer—to open us up to the universality of suffering. *Palestine is the Jewish story of today.* On the theological level, we need to acknowledge that we have left the era of post-Holocaust theology and have entered the era of post-Nakba theology. This is both

(July 29, 2007): http://www.jeremiahhaber.com/2007/07/no-rivkele-there-wasnt-roman-exile-of.html (accessed 8/24/16).

entirely theological and entirely political, because theology *is* politics and politics *is* theology.

Here is what you need to know about the Jewish community today: we are in big trouble. We have refused to acknowledge that we have become the oppressors, that we have fallen into exceptionalism and the idolatry of relying on military power, what liberation theologian Walter Wink names the "myth of redemptive violence."[1] The point here is that the Christian world is helping us to remain trapped in this sin out of its own need to expiate its guilt about Jewish suffering at the hands of the Christian West. The church has made anti-Semitism *the* Christian sin. If you are educated in seminary after World War II, this is what you learned. And in its zeal to cleanse Christian doctrine of the poison of anti-Jewishness, it has thrown the baby out with the bathwater and lost the core and the heart of the Gospels—which is the transformation of the prophetic tradition from the tribal to the universal. You can find the radical message of universal compassion in the Old Testament. Jesus quotes from Isaiah all the time—he is quoting Isaiah in that first

---

[1] See Walter Wink, "The Myth of Redemptive Violence," *The Bible in Transmission* (Spring 1999). Available online at: www2.goshen.edu/~joannab/women/wink99.pdf (accessed 8/1/16).*

sermon in Nazareth (Luke 4:16–30)—but it was Jesus who took the final, crucial step, declaring that the Temple is his body and on Pentecost sending his disciples out speaking all the languages of the world—including Arabic—to bring the good news that this is for all humankind.

Peter touched on the issue of covenant and promise yesterday. What about those promises in Genesis? It is in the covenant. There is a real-estate clause. The Old Testament is many things. I will not reduce it to one thing. It is many, many things and it is greater than the sum of its parts. Some parts of it are nationalist epics written and redacted at a time when particular kings were trying to consolidate power. One way it functions is to provide a narrative and theological rationale for nationalist aims. Walter Brueggemann writes much about the tension and ambiguity of the Old Testament around these critical issues of promise, land, and exclusivity.[1] Brueggemann is correct in describing a tension and an ambiguity about the tribal versus the universal. But I also see the tension as moving in a developmental direction in our

---

[1] See Walter Brueggemann, *Theology of the Old Testament: Testimony, Dispute, Advocacy* (Minneapolis: Fortress Press, 2005).*

understanding of God. It begins in Genesis, what I call God version 1.0: A family is chosen as the beginning of an epic describing God's plan for all of humankind. The story leads to a liberation from slavery, then to a conquest, then to a monarchy, then to a critique of that very monarchy. That's the prophets, that's version 1.5. Then fast forward to Jesus, calling for an end to temple, monarchy, and territoriality: version 2.0. Jesus was a radical Jew taking Judaism where it was supposed to go. It is a tragedy of history that Jews retreated back into insularity, into a sense of entitlement and hegemony and exceptionalism. Those other Jews following that Rabbi and that prophet and that community organizer, Jesus, started something new.

And now, out of the impulse—on its face a good and righteous impulse to reconcile with the Jewish people and cleanse Christianity of the poison of anti-Judaism, the church has betrayed not only Jesus, but the prophets, reverting to a theology that says that God *does* live on a mountain, *does* grant privilege to one particular people to occupy that mountain, *does* support a covenant that says God loves that people best, and that there is a real-estate clause in that covenant. I am talking here not about fundamentalist Christian Zionism, not about an End Times theology that maintains that Jewish hegemony in Palestine presages the Second Coming of Jesus, but the Christian Zionism that is hiding in plain sight in mainline, liberal Christianity—a belief in the Jewish right to the land that has nothing to do with that fundamentalist eschatology.[1]

When the Christian world confronted the ovens and said, "what have we done?" that was right. That was Western Christianity. That was an opportunity for Christians to look deep into themselves and ask what it about us that made this possible?

It takes some courage in the current climate for Christians to tell the truth about the Old Testament and to assert, without apology and boldly, that it is the Christian message, brought by that very good, revolutionary Jew, Jesus, that we must follow, whether we are Jew, Christian, Muslim, or claim no particular faith community or religion. Sadly, it is the Christians and their churches who have forgotten Jesus, who have in their haste to atone for church sins against the Jews, have forgotten his core message. There is much good in the Old Testament, it is the moral code of the Torah that Jesus is urging his people to follow, for the

---

[1] For more on this mainline, mainstream Christian Zionism, see Peter Miano's chapter in this volume.*

sake of their liberation from Roman oppression (the oppression helped by the Jewish authorities of the time), and it is the prophet Isaiah whom Jesus quotes from the beginning of his ministry in Nazareth—but despite its straining toward a universal humanitarianism, the Old Testament never steps out of an exclusivist tribal framework. It is Jesus who takes this step, calling for the destruction of the Temple, not so much in the physical but in the moral and spiritual sense.

Mainstream Christians did an end run around what was required by the confrontation with the ovens and stacked dead of the Nazi death camps. Christians avoided the recognition that it was Christian *exceptionalism* that laid the foundation for and promoted church anti-Semitism, thus preparing the ground for Hitler. Instead, because of this fixation on penitence for Christian sins against the Jews, Christians have re-granted that privilege and most beloved status to the Jews, in the bargain granting us the deed to the land, and in exchange joining in that "blessing" as the favored cousin. Christian exceptionalism has thus been replaced by Judeo-Christian exceptionalism, and its language is Zionism.

The issue surrounding Zionism and the status of the State of Israel is not anti-Semitism. It is racism. It is racism in the form of a colonial settler project that is guilty of humanitarian crimes, what Ilan Pappe has termed incremental genocide. We Jews face a crisis of monumental proportions, a matter of life or death. It is not unlike what Dietrich Bonhoeffer, confronting the crisis of his own German church in the 1930s, called a "reformation crisis."[1] We Jews are in spiritual peril. But this is our struggle, not yours.

Today the church is also in peril, as it was facing Nazism and as it was facing Apartheid South Africa. The church is facing a confessional crisis because of the Palestinian call and it must now tend to its own house in its response to the challenge of that call. It must not confuse the call of Palestine with the issue of its historical relationship to the Jews. That is a snare and a trap. It is being used to silence Christians. Christians must not allow it. Yes, if Christians stand up for the Palestinians they will be called anti-Semitic. Yes, the shameful church history of anti-Jewish doctrine and action will be thrown in their face, gently or otherwise. For many if not most liberal Christians, to be called anti-Semitic is the worst name you can be called. This

---

[1] See, for example, *Dietrich Bonhoeffer: Witness to Jesus Christ* (ed. John W. de Gruchy; Making of Modern Theology; Francisco: Collins, 1988).*

is your cross to pick up. Pick it up and let us move on. Is it really so heavy? This yoke is easy. This burden is light. It frees you to follow your faith and your consciences.

The church today is called again to stand up against racism, as it did a generation ago through the Ecumenical movement in the form of the Program to Combat Racism of the World Council of Churches in its stand against Apartheid South Africa and in its support for national liberation movements across the world. Today, that call comes in the duty to oppose the apartheid State of Israel as the tip of the iceberg of global economic and political oppression of the poor and most vulnerable. The challenge for the church today is not to allow its preoccupation with anti-Semitism to stand in the way of that duty.

Why is Palestine important? Because it represents structural violence (i.e., institutionalized racism, in its pure form). It is the successful establishment of an apartheid state, in our time, with the full support of the West, and the support of the institutional church. There is much theological work to do. This is a battle that is being waged on theological ground and on church ground.

This past June I was in Stuttgart, Germany, to attend the *Kirchentag.* Kirchentag is a huge, ecumenical church assembly held every two years. It is sponsored by the Protestant Church of Germany. This year, frustrated and unhappy with the Kirchentag's persistent refusal since 2009 to have any meaningful presentations about Palestine, the Christian-Palestine support network in Germany held their own alternative Kirchentag. They had to turn away people at the door. The 2009 Palestinian Kairos document presented a big problem for a church establishment firmly committed to support for the Jewish state. In 2011, the Middle East Committee of the German Protestant Church published its "Statement on Kairos Palestine" document.[1] Although recognizing the Palestinian document as a cry for help to the churches of the world, the German declaration clearly and explicitly showed itself to be unable to respond to that call. In fact, the document satisfies the criteria for Church theology laid out by the Kairos South Africa "Challenge to the Church" thirty years ago. However, rather than taking a prophetic stand against injustice by an oppressive state against a subject population, the authors of the declaration asked for "a more precise differentiation and definition of causes and

---

[1]   www.ccjr.us/dialogika-resources/themes-in-todays-dialogue/isrpal/1107-ekd2011aug31 (accessed 6/23/16).*

consequences" related to Palestinian suffering. In other words, they asked, "Don't we need more balance here?"[1] What about Palestinian violence? They chose to praise the Palestinian commitment to nonviolence, ignoring the violence of the State in pursuing its racist colonial program and in suppressing the resistance of the oppressed, both violent and nonviolent. It lifted up the idea of reconciliation, but in the service of supporting so-called "dialogue" and endless conversation as the crime of dispossession continues. This is false theology.

It is false theology for the authors of the Declaration to have come out against the Palestinian call for boycott of products made in the occupied Palestinian territories, because it "reminds the churches in Germany of the Nazi-appeal of 1933 'Do not buy from Jews!'"

Let me tell a quick story. It took me about a year and a half to find a publisher for my first book. In Germany it was snatched up in two months by a major publisher, because Germans are crazy for this issue. So, I was preparing for my first talk in Germany. I had never spoken to a German audience before. The guy who

---

[1]   www.kairossouthernafrica.wordpress.com/2011/05/08/the-south-africa-kairos-document-1985/ (accessed 6/23/16).*

organized knew what I was going to talk about. He came to me and said, "You know we are really glad you are here but please do me a favor and don't mention the boycott, because this is very upsetting for Germans." Well, you know what happened. I started off with this question: how many of you sitting here today do not understand the difference between the Palestinian call for boycott, divestment, and sanctions for Israel's human rights violations and the anti-Jewish laws of Nazi Germany in the 1930s? Their jaws dropped! *My God, he said that?* What I felt was gratitude, because I was speaking to their hearts and the burden the Germans carry and I was naming it. So, I proposed a deal to them. I said, if you stop seeing yourselves as the worse criminals in the history of the world, I will stop seeing myself as the worst victim in the history of the world. It is time to move on. Our souls, our psyches, and the fate of the world depends on this.

Have you seen Archbishop Tutu's "Open Letter to the German Evangelical Church Assembly"?[1] In typical Tutu style, with a twinkle in his eye—watch out for that twinkle!—he goes right for the hypocrisy and blindness

---

[1] See www.blog.eappi.org/2015/05/12/open-letter-from-archbishop-emeritus-desmond-tutu/ (accessed 6/23/16).*

of this argument, enjoining them to "Do business with Jews! Organize with them, love them. But don't support—militarily, economically or politically—the machinery of an apartheid state." "Beware of anti-Semitism," Tutu continues, "and all other forms of racism, but beware also of being cowed into silence by those who seek to stifle criticism of the oppressive politics of Israel by labeling you anti-Semitic." It is the same dynamic here in the U.S. Our preoccupation for anti-Semitism trumps our concern for justice and even US national interest!

It is also false theology when the German document objects to associating the Palestinian situation with the struggle against South African Apartheid because "it can lead to an ideological approach to the issue." In other words, don't mix this issue with politics. The objection to the South Africa analogy is common and is easily countered. Few who have witnessed the situation fail to make the connection. South Africans who have seen it say that it is worse than the apartheid that poisoned their country. What Israel is doing fits the definition of the crime of apartheid as ratified by the United Nations in

1973[1] and by the International Criminal Court meeting in Rome in 2002.[2] So why does the German church committee trouble itself to make this point? It is because once the word "apartheid" is uttered, the discourse enters "ideological" territory, because the speaker is talking about racism. And then people have little choice but to act.

John de Gruchy, one of the authors of the South African Kairos document, writing in the early 1980s, underscores this point, countering the argument that as a "religious" term heresy cannot be applied to apartheid: "The Christian faith has been misused in providing moral underpinning and theological legitimization to a racist ideology. In other words, it cannot be argued that apartheid is simply a political program unrelated to theology or the life of the

---

[1] See United Nations Resolution No. 14861, "International Convention on the Suppression and Punishment of the Crime of Apartheid. Adopted by the General Assembly of the United Nations on 30 November 1973." Available online at: www.treaties.un.org/doc/Publication/UNTS/Volume%201015/volume-1015-I-14861-English.pdf (accessed 8/1/16).*

[2] See "Rome Statute of the International Criminal Court." Available online at: www.icc-cpi.int/nr/rdonlyres/ea9aeff7-5752-4f84-be94-0a655eb30e16/0/rome_statute_english.pdf (accessed 8/1/16).*

Church."[1] The Dutch Reform Church explicitly provided the theological underpinning for apartheid. The German Lutheran Church ran headlong to embrace National Socialism, providing a civil religion and theologically and biblically based justification for Nazism.

Theology is political. It leads to action. *Church* theology is about *not acting*. Its proponents must find ways to deny and distort the truth, because when we acknowledge what is true, what is before our eyes, what Jesus in the Gospel of Luke means when he talks about reading "the signs of the times," then we must act.

It is this confession, this acknowledgment of racism as heresy that must motivate and drive our actions today. Any theology that serves to qualify or temporize on this point is false theology, because it serves to block action rather than to require it. A church in the grip of this theology is a church, in the words of South African author and theologian Charles Villa-Vicencio, "trapped in the dominant structures of

---

[1] John W. de Gruchy, "Towards a Confessing Church," *Apartheid is a Heresy* (ed. John W. de Gruchy and Charles Villa-Vicencio; Grand Rapids: Eerdmans, 1983), 75–93, here 82.*

oppression, controlled by entrenched bureaucracy, and conditioned by a history of compromise."[1]

Why, considering the global scale and reach of the crises confronting us, do we talk so much about Palestine? I have stood in the center of refugee camps in the Sudan that make Deheishe (a refugee camp in Bethlehem) look like a country club. If you want to talk about scale, there is far worse suffering in the world. That is not the point. Palestinian suffering represents structural violence. It is represented, financed, supported, and legitimized by most of the world. If we are silent on Palestine, how can we take on the urgent human rights issues in our own contexts? The converse is also true. Embracing the struggle of sisters and brothers outside of one's own context strengthens and grounds one's own struggle. Back in the twentieth century, the Ecumenical Movement named itself to underscore this reality. Martin Luther King, Jr. famously expresses this in his "Letter from a Birmingham Jail": "Injustice anywhere is a threat to justice everywhere. We are caught in an inescapable

---

[1] Charles Villa-Vicencio, *Trapped in Apartheid* (Maryknoll, NY: Orbis, 1988), 201.*

network of mutuality."[1] South African Anglican priest Rev. Edwin Arrison, head of Kairos Southern Africa, is fond of asking the question, "Who is the Palestinian in your backyard?"

The Church has done it before. The Church can do it again. Are we not back in Ottawa in 1982 at the conference of the World Alliance of Reformed Churches (WARC), when eight black and colored pastors publically refused to take communion with their white colleagues? We will not sit at the Lord's table with you, they announced, because we cannot do this with our white colleagues in Apartheid South Africa. In response, the WARC suspended the South African member churches and declared the global church body to be in *status confessionis:* nothing moves, all other church business takes a back seat, until this betrayal of the core values of our faith is addressed.[2] Are we not back in Uppsala, Sweden, in 1968, when the World Council of Churches named

---

[1] Martin Luther King, Jr. "Letter from a Birmingham Jail." Available online at: https://kinginstitute.stanford.edu/king-papers/documents/letter-birmingham-jail (accessed 8/1/16).*

[2] This event is one of 23 events highlighted in the 150-year history of WARC—and one of only seven events highlighted since 1980 on the WARC's official website. See "History of WARC." Available online at: http://wcrc.ch/history/history-of-the-world-communion-of-reformed-churches (accessed 8/1/16).*

confronting racism as the primary mission of the church? Are we not back in Montgomery in 1955? Remember what Martin Luther King wrote in the "Letter from a Birmingham Jail"? He wrote that our stumbling block is not the Ku Klux Klan or the White Citizen's Council. It was the white moderate who preferred a "peace without conflict to a peace with justice."

If Apartheid is a heresy because it is racism, then is not Zionism a heresy because it is racism, and so is not the church's obligation TO SAY THIS, and to declare itself in *status confessionis*? And does not this lead directly to the requirement for the church to speak and to act globally? We are here again.

The question is sometimes asked, what would Jesus do if he were to come back to Jerusalem today? He would stand on the Mount of Olives, shed a few tears, but then waste no time proceeding straightaway into West Jerusalem, to the Knesset building, the seat of the Israeli government, a government tragically and sinfully devoted to the destruction of Palestinian civilization and to the establishment of racist colonial rule over the remaining Palestinians in what is now Israel, a single apartheid state from the river to the sea. He would stand in front of the Knesset and say "Destroy this temple!" And you know that Jesus would not be talking about violence or "terrorism," about bombs or the methods of war. He would be demanding, as he did two thousand years ago, and as the prophets did before him, the transformation of the evil system into a rule of equality and compassion. He would be proclaiming the Kingdom.

The world is full of these temples. They are the governments and the church institutions supporting these governments in their sinful and oppressive practices. We must celebrate those leaders of the past: Black liberation leaders in the USA, the South African anti-Apartheid leaders, liberation theologians and clergy working and dying for social justice in Latin America, and people all over the world, on every continent, who make up the emerging Kairos movement.

I don't have any conversations about the two-state solution or the one-state solution. That discussion is over. We have one State. It is called Israel. It is an apartheid State. It is not up to us to decide what the future looks like. It is our job to say "No" to apartheid Israel. Our job is to do for Israel what the Church did for apartheid South Africa.

A New Dictionary for Palestine
Calling a Spade a Spade
Ilan Pappe

It is a great pleasure to take part in this important conference and to share the podium with so many able speakers. In fact, the work of fellow presenters is so invigorating and their contributions are on such a high level that they are a very difficult act to compare with. I hope that I can maintain as high as a standard they are setting forth.

I would like to speak, as I promised in the title, of the need to use a new language when we discuss or when we are engaged with Palestine. This is not really a new language. The entries in the dictionary that I would like us all to consider have been written long before our time—and some of the language I would like to practice has been used by others before, but it seldom enters the hegemonic dictionary or vocabulary of the peace activists when the issue of Palestine was and is discussed. I do not think that people who have been active for Palestine for many years would object to some of the entries in the new dictionary that I would propose. I am sure they do not. My point is not that they object to them. My point is that they are not using them frequently enough. And if activists do not use these words or concepts frequently enough, then others who are less committed or less engaged with the question are not likely to use them at all. Some of the leading activists for the cause of Palestine in the West and in Israel actually reject some of the entries I would suggest today. So, maybe that is another reason why the kind of language I would like to see employed when we describe or analyze Palestine or when we talk about the vision for Palestine, maybe this is another reason why people find it hard to employ these kinds of language, discourse, or concepts.

Ideological Preamble to Lexicographical Revisions

I thought that in order to illuminate such a new dictionary I would concentrate on three concepts that in my mind have to be at the center of our conversation on Palestine. I find it very useful to connect these three entries to the three major rights of the Palestinians that I think we are all struggling for or have been struggling for many years. I think we became aware again of these three basic rights that

Palestinians do not enjoy since the emergence of the Boycott, Divestment, and Sanctions movement (BDS).[1] The BDS has a consensus around three rights of the Palestinians that have to be respected, and if they are not respected, there is a moral imperative to boycott and divest from Israel—and hopefully convince governments to sanction it in the future. These three rights are connected to three different concepts and ideas that I think we have to refresh and talk about. But before I do that, I would like to say that this is not just a linguistic challenge. This is not suggesting a word for a word or an entry for an entry. It is also a discussion about an analysis (i.e., a perception) that lies at the heart of the two approaches to peace and reconciliation in Israel and Palestine.

There is a genuine conversation between two points of view that coexist within a genuine movement of solidarity with the Palestinian people. I am not comparing the Israeli perspective with the Palestinian perspective. I am talking about two perspectives that emerged in the last thirty or forty years within the solidarity movement with the Palestinians that also reflect debates within the Palestinian national

---

[1] For information on the DBS movement, see https://bdsmovement.net/ (accessed 7/29/16).*

movement itself and among the peace camp in Israel. These are not disconnected. We do not call it a debate, because the solidarity movement with the Palestinians is as fragile as such movements can get. Fragile movements are not likely to air out debates, because they do not want to weaken the struggle. Sometimes, though, if you do not discuss openly what disunites you, it comes back with a vengeance. I think it is good even among friends and family members to discuss openly and genuinely differences of opinion.

And the two different paradigms are as follows: There is the paradigm that views the conflict in Palestine as a conflict between two nationalist movements. This point of view does not want to enter discussions about whether Judaism could be nationalism or whether the idea of partitioning Palestine is morally unacceptable. That is, not only the question of whether it is practical or not, but whether it should be discussed at all. As you know, for instance, the two communist parties on both sides of the divide, who were very powerful and important political forces before 1948 (of course they are hardly visible today, but were very important in the past) were strongly supporting the idea of partitioning Palestine and supporting the perception of the conflict as a conflict between two legitimate national movements.

The whole idea of liberal Zionism—or what we call the Israeli peace camp—was based on the assumption that the *quid pro quo* for recognizing the rights of the Palestinians was a demand from the Palestinians to recognize the rights of the Jews to have a nation-state in Palestine. Therefore, the whole question was merely where that Israeli nation-state would be and what the partition line would be. In any event, there was an assumption of some kind of parity between two legitimate national movements that happened to find themselves in a long, ongoing, and bloody conflict that needed the presence of an external mediator to reconcile the two sides, because the two sides could not do that on their own. This was the basis of the American peace process; it was the basis of the Oslo process. This is more or less the agenda of quite a few of the solidarity groups with the Palestinian people, especially from the late 1980s when the official Palestinian leadership, the PLO, more or less accepted, with some grudges and reservations, these underlying assumptions as the paradigm for peace. So, persons organizing and working under these assumptions would demonstrate for a two-state solution. They would demonstrate for the creation of an independent Palestinian state and they would pressure their government to recognize the Palestinian state in its parliament. And this is one paradigm.

There is a different paradigm and one that I subscribe to and one that I think demands a different language—a different dictionary. This second paradigm says this is not a conflict between two nationalist movements. This is a conflict between a settler, colonialist movement that came to Palestine long after the classical colonialist movements had come to an end. This is a project in work. It is still going on. The colonization of Palestine has not ended. It continues on a daily basis and peace is not reconciling between two nationalist movements, it is asking yourself in the present, can there be a legitimate, successful, and just anti-colonialist struggle in the land of Palestine? The question is not, what does peace mean? The question is, what does decolonization mean in the contemporary setting?

We had a glimpse of what decolonization means in South Africa in the late 1980s. There was no attempt to reconcile two nationalist movements in South Africa. Although the language was about Apartheid, about one person/one vote, about democracy in South Africa, historically, it was much more than that. It was an attempt to bring to closure the settler-colonialist project of South Africa that began in the seventeenth century, where people ran away from Europe and colonized a part of Africa. First, they were aided by the British Empire and then they fought against the British Empire. Eventually, they strove to keep their settler-colonialist possession through the system of Apartheid and other related tools of colonialism. By the mid-1980s, most of the civilized world regarded settler-colonialism in South Africa as illegal, immoral, and unacceptable. In the contemporary setting, some of the greatest supporters of the Palestinian cause refuse to accept that Israel is a similar settler-colonialist project that has to be treated in the same way that South Africa was.

Alterations to Our Dictionary Regarding Israel-Palestine

Now there are three entries to the dictionary that I hope will illustrate this point even further, and I believe they are connected to the campaign of Boycott, Divestment, and Sanction. The first term that I think is redundant and not useful is the term *occupation*. I understand when you live in Ramallah and you use the Arabic word for occupation, you know exactly what you mean and you cannot dispense of this term, because it means a very close proximity to the Israeli military presence, it means that basically the only

Israelis you meet are soldiers or that you frequently see the might of the Israeli army at close hand. Of course, in the Gaza strip, this is even more true than it is for the West Bank, since 2006. But there is something about this term, occupation, that provides a shield of immunity to the State of Israel. One has to realize that the term "occupation" is not just a descriptive concept that is used to analyze the presence of a foreign power in someone else's homeland. The term also has international, legal implications. It has philosophical implications. Usually occupation has to do with temporary means. It has a beginning and an end. Most of the international law that you know about occupation was drafted at a time when foreign powers were occupying another country with the very certain knowledge that this occupation would last no more than four or five years. So, they asked themselves, what can we do, legally, while we occupy this territory? International law that deals with occupation was established to protect the occupied people and the occupier for a very limited period of time.

If one looks at the discourse of Israeli politicians since 1967, one can see how the temporary nature of occupation is used brilliantly to fend off any pressure on the State of Israel. The Israeli authorities continue to say that this is a temporary situation, so even if the protestors are correct and Israeli occupation of Palestine does violate basic human rights, the Israeli authorities are able to object that the occupation is just a temporary measure, pending a peace agreement, pending a solution, pending a settlement. Furthermore, because it is considered a temporary occupation, one cannot criticize the Israelis for allowing the army to be the sovereign in the occupied territories. Thus, on the one hand, even peace activists of the type described in the first paradigm can persuade themselves that they do not want to see Israeli civilian law in the occupied territories, because that would mean annexation and normalization of the colonization. Yet, on the other hand, for Palestinians who have been under the hands of the Israeli army for 50 years, would it really be worse to be under Israeli civilian law? Don't misunderstand me. Neither Israeli civilian nor military law are good for Palestinians.

For perspective, please reconsider the validity of the term "occupation" after fifty years. Israel without occupation existed less than twenty years. Israel with occupation is more than fifty years old. So, does the language of "occupation," implicitly a temporary phenomenon, really correlate to the realities on the ground in the West Bank and Gaza? I would answer, "No!" This is not occupation. In fact, no central Israeli political figure has ever conceived the presence of the Israeli army or settlements in either the West Bank or Gaza as occupation. For them, it was the completion of the settler-colonialist project that was begun in the late nineteenth century. What they did not succeed to do in 1948, they hoped to complete in 1967.

The moment that people understand that the Israelis could not do in 1967 what they did in 1948, namely, ethnically cleanse the people of the West Bank as they ethnically cleansed most of Palestine in 1948, the situation and the use of "occupation" becomes a far more complicated reality. The Israelis cannot, then, impose the law as they did in the areas occupied in 1967 in the same fashion as they did in the lands they occupied in 1948. But from our perspective as activists, if we decide to differentiate between the occupation of the Galilee in 1948 and the occupation of Hebron in 1967, if we do that in our minds, we are missing the fact that the fifty years that have passed since the occupation of Jericho and the seventy years since the occupation of Haifa are meaningless from a historical perspective. So, the only difference between the two places is that one was occupied fifty years ago and the other was occupied seventy years ago.

Of course, people say, "But the international community recognized the occupation of 1948 and does not recognize the occupation of 1967." It is only when one has lived in Israel all one's life, as I have, that one understands how insignificant the distinction between 1948 and 1967 is from an Israeli point of view. The Israelis have learned that what matters is what happens on the ground, not the language about what happens on the ground. Namely, if the Israelis employ the right language, if they can be a juggler of words, if they can launder the words, they make one occupation seem to be temporary (i.e., since 1967), and the other one (since 1948) seem to be legitimate. Already, according to most pragmatic leaders of the West Bank, part of what we call the occupation of the West Bank is recognized as officially part of Israel. So, if we insist on the language of colonization, if we insist on depicting the Israeli actions in the West Bank and Gaza as part of the settler-colonialist project, then we will be able to show that there is no difference in the motivation, planning, or vision behind Israeli actions in Jerusalem, Gaza, the West Bank, or Galilee. The ideological origin is the same. The objective is the same. The means employed are the same. Yet, even in the peace movement, we have unwisely adopted different language to describe activities inside the green line and outside the green line. The language of occupation should be replaced with the language of *colonialism*.

The second concept that we should use much more frequently and with greater force, after the idea of colonialism, involves the way we describe the rights that are abused by Israel within the green line (i.e., in Israel proper). I know that we are beginning to use the word "apartheid" more and more with regard to Israel itself. I think this is an important entry in the new dictionary, i.e., using the word *apartheid*. Now, scholars would tell you, and rightly so, that if you compare historically, legally, politically, and even economically, the two systems (i.e., the Israeli and South African systems), there are many differences. But, politically, conceptually, they are very similar. We can understand what is particular in the apartheid system that Israel has established inside the green line, the kinds of laws and practices that Israel has promoted in the last ten years, and have a clear ideological origin behind them.

For example, in the Galilee there are about sixty Jewish neighborhoods. They have been built incrementally since 1948—usually on expropriated Palestinian land. According to law in Israel, Palestinian citizens of Israel cannot live in those neighborhoods. I am talking about a legal procedure that allows a community that is built as a public community not to accept other citizens of the State as part of the community because of their national or religious or ethnic identity. This by itself should locate Israel very close to Apartheid South Africa in the table of rogue states. Yet, this has not been part of the peace discourse, because this happens inside Israel. It is not the West Bank. It is not Gaza. So, talking about apartheid as part of our regular discussion of Israel-Palestine and the practices there in terms of the settler-colonialist project is very important as part of a more concentrated and focused language to describe what is wrong in Israel-Palestine.

The last new entry in the dictionary is related to the third right that BDS wants to protect. It is the right of the refugees to return to Palestine. Politically, the Palestinian leadership long ago essentially removed any meaningful right of return from peace negotiations, but then again, there are not any meaningful peace negotiations. It is not so much the right of return that I am speaking of, although this must be part of the discourse. Rather I am referring to the idea I wrote about in my 2007 book.[1] This idea is that Israel is consciously and intentionally using **ethnic cleansing** as part of their central understanding of Zionism. Removing the Palestinians from Palestine is not the byproduct of Zionism. It is the main preoccupation of Zionism as an ideological system. More than 100,000 Israeli strategists, politicians, clerics, civil servants, and military people are daily engaged with how to downsize the number of Palestinians who live in historical Palestine. These people are daily engaged in this very basic objective of eliminating or removing Palestinians from historical Palestine. The Israelis need this vast number of people dedicated to the task of de-Palestinianizing Palestine, because they cannot now do what they did in 1948. Today, they cannot very easily remove one million people *en masse* and still claim to be part of the civilized world. As a center of international media, the Israelis—thank God!—have some inhibitions.

But, there are other means of achieving the dislocation of the Palestinian people—as witnessed by contemporary Israeli national strategy and national interest. When Israelis talk about national interest, it

---

[1] Ilan Pappe, *The Ethnic Cleansing of Palestine* (Reprint ed.; New York: OneWorld Publications, 2007).*

means they are going back to their desks to see how many Palestinian babies were born in the past year. And whether the natural growth of both communities is changing.[1] This is the real Israeli obsession with strategic national thinking. It is not the Iranian bomb threat. Every senior Israeli official—the head of the Mossad, the head of the army, strategic think tanks—will tell you that there was never a worry about an Iranian nuclear weapon. They are not worried about it now. They understand that it was used as a distraction and that it was needed by the Israeli government to legitimate domestic objectives. When you talk to them about the number of Palestinians who are still within what is regarded as the space of the Jewish State, then they will tell you that this is a serious threat. It is considered an issue of survival. This is an existential threat. That is the truth that has to be exposed. It is incredible, but if you think that the worst that can happen to a Palestinian is being bombed in Gaza or being detained in the West Bank, also give your

---

[1] See, for example, Bennett Zimmerman and Michael Wise, "Defusing the Demographic Time Bomb," *Jewish Policy Center: Contemporary Conservative Thought* (Spring 2008). Available online at: http://www.jewishpolicycenter.org/2008/02/29/defusing-the-demographic-time-bomb/ (accessed 7/12/16).*

thoughts and your prayers to those who live within the Israeli State where every time a Palestinian baby is born he or she is considered to be a demographic bomb.

It is not surprising that a lot of people in Haifa claim that that they feel liberated when they go to Ramallah. This is because Haifa is part of the charade of the Israeli democracy. In Haifa, the gap between how Palestinians are really perceived by their Jewish neighbors, by the Israeli politicians and by the Israeli secret service and how they are viewed by the world as the "lucky Palestinians" (because they live in the only democracy in the Middle East) is vivid and poignant. For some people, this gap is even more unbearable and demoralizing than living under direct occupation. People can be liberated from occupation, but how is one liberated from life in a reality show that portrays Palestinian Israelis as living in the only democracy in the Middle East while the Israeli secret service is monitoring how many babies they have? Every Palestinian—regardless of where that Palestinian lives—is viewed as a threat because the Israeli authorities are determined to avoid breaching the thirty-percent demographic threshold of Palestinians living within Israel proper. Anything above thirty percent is deemed as a grave existential threat to Israel.

One might well ask, "So why don't they look at the map as a whole and see that between the Mediterranean and the River Jordan there is already a Jewish minority?" But in the settler-colonialist mindset, there are different means to downsize the (Palestinian) population. After all, according to most Israeli textbooks, according to common Israeli ideology, and according to the Zionist Israeli vision of what is most hoped for in life, those Palestinians should not be there in the first place. Of course, one does not have to expel all of the unwanted population in order for them to disappear. Rather, they can be put in enclaves. They can be ghettoized.

I have mentioned these three points: (1) that we substitute talk of competing nationalisms with talk of a settler-colonialist project; (2) that we substitute talking about occupation with talk about colonization; and (3) that we substitute talk of a peace process with the language of ethnic cleansing. And, in closing I will mention another. I refuse to talk about Israel's right to exist. Rather, I am eager to talk about regime change. I am very willing to participate in discussions about whether the regime in Israel and Palestine should change. Should we strive to create a different economic, political, legal, and moral reality between the Jordan River and the Mediterranean? For this, I am very willing to participate in those conversations, but not about Israel's right to exist. That is why regime change is so important. There twelve million people in this area, half of whom have no say in their own future, no elections in which to express their ideas, and no way to take part in decision making. Even in Israel, Palestinians do not take part in any serious decision making, not to mention the refugees who have no voice in any political system. So, in order to change the game, we need to change the perception of what is Palestine. Is Palestine only the West Bank and Gaza? Are the Palestinians only the people who live there?

Now, I am not naïve and I don't expect senior politicians to start talking about Zionism as colonialism, about Israel as an apartheid state, about the Palestinian refugees as the victims of ethnic cleansing and that the only way to rectify what happened to them is by repatriation. I do not expect senior Israeli politicians to use the new dictionary, but I think all of us should. Especially, in academia, when we talk about colonialism, we should examine Israel. When we have a course about apartheid, Israel should be included. When ethnic cleansings and genocide in the twentieth century are discussed, we should include Israel. This is very important, because it is about freedom of expression within academia. Alternative media are already doing it. But there is no alternative academia. And, you know, "courageous academics" is a bit of an oxymoron.

We need to teach that Israel is a case study that is not unique, not exceptional in what it did or what it does. But Israel should be considered within the correct framework. It is not part of the book of the history of democracy. Israel should not be featured in the book about human rights legislation. It should not be featured in any course about civilized societies. We should relocate it into the historical, conceptual, and ideological framework where it would be discussed with the other examples of human rights violations, civil rights violations, and injustices, with the hope that it would feed back to what we used to call the peace process. Because what we need is not a peace process. We need to decolonize all of Palestine to have a regime that is democratic for all and to have a just system that would justify the concept of a holy land for all of us.

Can the United States "Manage" the Middle East? Should It Try?

Stephen Walt

The central focus of this conference is Israel-Palestine, and the role of Christians, but this needs to be put into a broader context and that is what I will try to do. As the title of this lecture suggests, I intend to speak on United States policy in the greater Middle East and not just Israel-Palestine. If the question is: "Can the US manage the Middle East?" Today's headlines would seem to give a pretty clear answer—No! Heck no! Indeed, there is a widespread sense that the whole place is going to hell in a handbasket and that the United States is either unwilling or unable to do anything to improve the situation.

There is no great mystery why people have doubts about this now. We have a near-failed state in Iraq after a long and costly occupation. We have the so-called Islamic State doing gruesome things and resisting efforts to degrade and destroy it. There is the grinding civil war in Syria, with about 200,000 killed so far and no end in sight. A unified Syria may never reemerge. Another civil war in Yemen after two decades of repeated United States interference there. There is a failed state in Libya with near chaos and civil war. The Arab Spring is turning into Arab winter in Egypt, with the US once again backing a thuggish military dictatorship with few redeeming features. The Israeli-Palestinian peace process is essentially dead. The prospects for a two-state solution, which was the formally stated goal of last three United States presidents, is probably over. Certainly it is nowhere in sight. One piece of good news is that we have an agreement on Iran's nuclear program, but we should bear in mind that it is not as good a deal as we could have gotten several years ago and many people are still trying to find ways to derail it. There is an escalating split between Sunni and Shia Muslims, rising radicalism, and the plight of Christians and other minorities is increasingly bleak.

The United States obviously is not responsible for all of these developments, but we did play a big role in many of them. What I'm going to do today is try to explain why we are having such trouble and point the way to a different approach. To do that, I will first identify what I think are the United States's interests in the Middle East. Then, I will provide a brief sketch of the evolution of United States policy over the past fifty years or so, highlighting recent failures in the Middle East. I will try to explain why we keep having such trouble and suggest a different way to proceed by NOT trying to manage the Middle East.

So what are the interests of the United States? I think we have three main *strategic* interests, and there is not a lot of disagreement about these interests in Washington. First, there is access to energy, i.e., making sure that energy from the Middle East continues to flow out to world markets. Despite the shale/gas revolution, this is still a strategic interest. Second, we have an interest in preventing the proliferation of weapons of mass destruction. This has been a general goal for a long time, though the United States has not been entirely consistent, because we have long turned a blind eye to Israel's nuclear arsenal, an important exception, but it is still a goal elsewhere in region. A third interest is to limit or prevent anti-American terrorism, especially since 9/11.

In addition, there are a couple of moral commitments or moral interests that we have had in the region. First, the United States has had a moral commitment to Israel as homeland for Jewish people and as a democracy, but of course as you have already heard, that moral case is not nearly as clear-cut as it once was, given the long Israeli occupation and its brutal treatment of Palestinians. Yet it still carries at least some weight in the American political system. A second moral interest is that we would like to promote democracy and human rights; this often takes a back seat to other interests whenever they come into conflict. Finally, I think that the United States has a basic strategic and humanitarian interest in peace in general.

One observation is that none of these goals requires the United States to control the Middle East or to turn it into a replica of the United States of America. In fact, trying to do that provokes hostile reactions, makes terrorism worse and proliferation of weapons of mass destruction more likely. So mostly the United States has tried to *manage* the Middle East. The question is, how?

As most people acknowledge, the US didn't pay much attention to the Middle East before 1945. The US was involved in education and missionary work, but mostly we left the Middle East to Britain and France. I might add that the image of the US in the region through 1945 was very positive. The United States was seen as benevolent and, importantly, *not imperialist.* According to Louise Fawcett of Oxford University, before 1945 the US was "popular and respected throughout the region. Americans were seen as good people, untainted by the selfishness and duplicity associated with the Europeans."[1]

During the Cold War, the US acted like an *offshore balancer.* The US had significant security ties with a number of regional powers. The US was actively involved in regional diplomacy. But the US did not station forces in regions or intervene in the Middle East for lengthy periods of time. The US intervened in Lebanon 1958, but briefly, and in 1983, but again the US got out quickly. After the Shah of Iran fell in 1979, the US created the Rapid Deployment Force, but kept it over-the-horizon and out of the region. The US tended to play a balance-of-power game—tilting toward Saddam Hussein in the 1980s when he was fighting Iran and turning *against* Iraq after Saddam's invasion of Kuwait. The key is that at this time, the US was actively involved in the region, but not permanently intervening and not staging large military forces there. This policy was not perfect, but on the whole it worked pretty well and the US managed to

---

[1] Louise Fawcett, *The International Relations of the Middle East* (New York: Oxford University Press, 2005), 284.*

achieve most of its Middle East goals, though its image in most of the region declined steadily.

The first big change came after the First Gulf War in 1991. Instead of ending that war and withdrawing, the US left substantial military forces in the Gulf and adopted a policy under President Bill Clinton of *dual containment*. Instead of using Iraq and Iran to balance each other, we pledged to contain both of them simultaneously. This policy was widely criticized at the time as strategically foolish, but according to Martin Indyk and Ken Pollack of the Brookings Institute, dual containment was undertaken to reassure Israel and try and make Israel more compliant in Oslo process.[1] Alas, presence of American forces in Saudi Arabia led Osama Bin Laden to focus on what he called "the far enemy" and thus dual containment played a key role in bringing about the September 11 attacks. The bottom line is that dual containment was a strategic blunder.

---

[1] For detailed analysis, see Kenneth M. Pollack, Daniel L. Byman, Martin Indyk, et al., "Which Path to Persia? Options for a New American Strategy toward Iran," *Analysis Paper* 20 (Washington, DC: Saban Center for Middle East Policy at the Brookings Institution, 2009). Available online at: http://www.brookings.edu/~/media/research/files/papers/2009 /6/iran-strategy/ 06_ iran_strategy.pdf (accessed 5/16/16).*

The US also acted as so-called mediator during the Oslo process, but the Clinton Administration bungled the job. Instead of being evenhanded, the US acted as "Israel's lawyer"—to use Aaron David Miller's phrase[1]—and did essentially nothing as the number of settlers in the West Bank doubled between 1993 and 2000. The US also mishandled the Camp David summit in 2000, which made things even worse. So dual containment and the Oslo Process didn't work out very well, but although it might be hard to believe, the next phase was even more inept.

After the September 11 attacks, President Bush, Vice-President Dick Cheney, and the neoconservatives adopted a strategy of regional transformation beginning with the invasion of Iraq in 2003. Their goal was to demonstrate American power; to intimidate, coerce, and topple potential foes there; and to produce regime change in Iraq, Syria, and then Iran, creating a sea of pro-American democracies, and thereby reducing the terror threat and leaving Israel more secure.

---

[1] See Aaron David Miller, "Israel's Lawyer," *The Washington Post* (May 23, 2005). Available online at: www.washingtonpost.com/wpdyn/content/article/2005/05/22/AR2005052200883.html (accessed 5/16/16).*

Now, when one steps back and thinks about this today, this whole idea sounds ludicrous, even delusional, but lots of smart, well-educated, and influential people swallowed it one-hundred percent. It was an amazing moment of national insanity.

You all know the results: a failed state, civil war, and insurgency in Iraq and increased Iranian influence there, which is not what the neocons envisioned. Meanwhile, throughout this period no progress was made whatsoever on Israel-Palestine. The Bush team at one point promoted the so-called Road Map. The Road Map never went anywhere and Bush continued to let Israel expand settlements with essentially no limits. The result was that Hamas became more popular and a two-state solution became less and less likely, which brings us to President Obama's presidency.

I would characterize the Obama administration's policy with four *Ds*: diplomacy, disengagement, drones, and democracy. *Diplomacy* is the outreach to the Arab and Muslim world manifested in the Cairo speech at the beginning of Obama's presidency,[1] along with repeated efforts to try to

---

[1] See "Remarks by the President at Cairo University," The White House (June 4, 2009). Available online at:

restart the Israel-Palestine peace process and get to the two-state solution. The second D is *Disengagement* from Iraq and Afghanistan, and wariness of big military operations. President Obama learned the lesson of Iraq. This Obama policy is a partial return to an earlier period. But with the increased reliance on *Drones*, the use of special forces, and air power, the US has become active in more places under President Obama than it was under President Bush, but with smaller and more discrete tools of military force. Finally, we come to *Democratization,* which Obama explicitly endorsed in the Cairo speech. Initially, President Obama saw the Arab Spring as a promising development. The US helped nudge Mubarak out in Egypt. The US actively helped topple Moamar Gaddafi in Libya, but the US did not intervene in Syria and ignored the Saudi Arabian-backed repression in Bahrain.

Incidentally, the US did not foresee the emergence of ISIS at any point nor did it anticipate the Houthi rebellion in Yemen, but responded with US airstrikes and by supporting Saudi Arabia's campaign in Yemen.

---

www.whitehouse.gov/the-press-office/remarks-president-cairo-university-6-04-09 (accessed 7/29/16).*

Needless to say, with the exception of the Iran deal, the results of the past three presidents have been disappointing—Republicans and Democrats alike. There is no two-state solution. The rest of the region is going from bad to worse. The image of the US in the region is lower than it was at end of Bush Administration.

So the question is: why have three very different presidents done so poorly, despite enormous US power and its mostly benevolent intentions?

Why does the US keep screwing up?

One obvious problem is that we have pursued the wrong goals on several occasions. Dual containment was obviously a bone-headed strategy. Trying to spread democracy at the point of a gun and assuming it could be done quickly and cheaply was delusional. Everything we know about democratic transitions suggests they are very difficult, they take a long time; and this is especially true in states with deep divisions within their societies and a lack of democratic traditions. Yet the US plunged ahead, convinced it would be easy to do this in places like Iraq and Libya.

The US spent ten years trying to get Iran to give up its entire nuclear enrichment program, while refusing to talk to them. The result was that Iran went from zero nuclear centrifuges operating in the year 2000 to between 11,000 and 20,000 in September 2015. That number will be rolled back as a result of the nuclear agreement, but not to the point it was in 2000 when the US was refusing to have any diplomatic contact with Iran whatsoever.

Another problem has been strategic contradictions. Even when the US sought sensible goals, it often implemented policies that undermined them. The US was committed to a two-state solution in Israel-Palestine and also to unconditional support for Israel. This is a contradiction, because a two-state solution is not possible unless there is willingness to pressure both sides. The US was committed to preventing Iran from gaining nuclear weaponry, yet the US repeatedly threatened Iran with military force and regime change. Well, if your goal is to convince a country that it does not need a nuclear deterrent, threatening to overthrow its government is not the best approach. The US wanted to limit anti-American terrorism, yet it helped dismantle several authoritarian states that were actually not bad at controlling terrorism, and it continued to support local governments—both Arab and non-Arab—whose policies are making the problem of terrorism worse. Finally, the US continues to meddle in these societies, even though there is lots of evidence suggesting that *jihadi* terrorism is heavily motivated by opposition to foreign interference. So we should not be surprised by repeated failures.

A third problem is that the US simply does not understand the region of the Middle East very well and it is not particularly patient. Since the 1990s, the US has increasingly found itself trying to manipulate the internal politics of these countries and do, for lack of a better term, nation-building. But the US lacked the expertise to do this well. It is hard enough to manage politics in places we understand well—like here in the US—but it is exceedingly difficult to manage in places where detailed knowledge is lacking. The US got hoodwinked by Ahmed Chalabi, for example, who told the US lies about what was happening in Iraq and the US did not know enough to know that he was lying. The US did not understand Iraqi politics, so it ran an inept occupation. The US does not know how to pick reliable partners, because it does not know the individual people well enough. The US has been repeatedly played by leaders like Saleh in Yemen, who pretended to be allies in the "war on terror," but who were just using us to advance their own agendas. The US had no idea what to do in Libya after ousting Gaddafi. The result is the worst of all possible worlds. Local populations see us as interfering all the time. This fuels conspiracy theories—yet our interventions don't succeed.

A further problem is that the US continues using the wrong tools. Specifically, the US is trying to use military power to solve what are essentially political problems. The US has the world's largest hammer. It is not surprising that the whole world looks like a nail. Military force is a very crude instrument. It is not good at political solutions. It has lots of unintended consequences. No one can predict all of its effects. Drone strikes are a perfect example. The US has killed plenty of suspected terrorists, along with hundreds of innocent civilians. The result of this is that local populations turn against us, making the problem of terrorism worse, rather than better. US reliance on violence invites the response by our opponents and this tends to bring to prominence people who are good at violence and those who enjoy violence and are adept at it. This is not the way to build stable, peaceful, and effective societies. The US's other big tool is money, but money is also a crude instrument. It does not give as much leverage as we think it will. Pouring money into different countries fuels corruption, allows bad leaders to remain in power, but does not necessarily produce the desired results.

Another problem is that US policy is undermined by the so-called *special relationships* with Israel and Saudi Arabia. As numerous leaders in the region have acknowledged and numerous scholarly studies have shown, anger at the plight of Palestinians remains a touchstone in the Arab world, an inspiration to radical extremists, and a serious problem for US policy. Israel also takes up enormous bandwidth in the US foreign policy agenda. Look at all the time and attention Secretary John Kerry and President Obama spend on a country with a population less than that of New York City. And do they get thanked for their efforts? Heavens, no. Of course, the US's special relationship with Saudi Arabia is no better. Its political system is completely contrary to US values. Wealthy Saudis continue to fund Islamic extremists. Neither is Saudi Arabia exactly a compliant ally despite getting US protection.

A final reason the US has such a poor track record in the Middle East is that we keep recycling the same failed policies and officials into key policymaking jobs, while expecting different results. Dennis Ross and Martin Indyk, for example, had eight years to get a peace deal during 1990s under the most favorable circumstances anyone could have imagined. They failed completely, yet both were rehired by President

Obama to do exactly the same thing and they achieved exactly the same results yet again. Similarly, Elliot Abrams, who was convicted for lying to Congress during the 1980s, was pardoned by the first President Bush and then reappointed by the second President Bush, helped Ariel Sharon derail the Road Map and then screwed up Gaza by trying to foment a Fatah-led coup against Hamas. Upon leaving government, Abrams was appointed as senior fellow on the Council of Foreign Relations, thereby demonstrating that no amount of incompetence in foreign policy disqualifies a person from continued involvement in foreign policy formation. Not everyone dealing with Middle East policy has done this badly, but picking Middle East personnel mostly to keep the Israel lobby happy doesn't seem to be producing successful outcomes.

So, what about the Israel lobby? The Israel lobby is a loose coalition of individuals and organizations, such as AIPAC (The American Israel Public Affairs Committee), working openly to promote a special relationship between the US and Israel.[1] By "special relationship," I mean one in which the US gives

---

[1]See John J. Mearsheimer and Stephen M. Walt, *The Israel Lobby and U.S. Foreign Policy* (New York: Farrar, Straus and Giroux, 2007).*

Israel essentially unconditional support, such as economic, military, and diplomatic protection, regardless of what Israel does. The Israel lobby is not a cabal. It is not a conspiracy. It does not control every aspect of US Middle East policy. For example, AIPAC could not prevent the Iran deal.

Indeed, I think a good case can be made that the Israel lobby has become slightly less effective over time than it used to be. Israel's own conduct is much harder to defend. It is not as much of a strategic asset as it might have been during the Cold War. Israel's occupation and repeated wars against Palestinians have tarnished its image badly. In the twenty-first century, it is just very hard to defend apartheid. That is, in effect, what the lobby now has to do. Some issues—and the Iran deal fits here perfectly—are especially hard for AIPAC to win, especially in the aftermath of the Iraq war. Remember that the only alternative to the Iran deal, as Professor Chomsky points out in this volume, was either an Iran that had no constraints on its nuclear program whatsoever or military force. So, given three choices—a pretty good, though imperfect deal, or an unconstrained Iranian nuclear program, or a war—it is pretty clear which choice makes the most sense. This means AIPAC and other opponents to the deal did not have very good cards to play. So, President Obama could beat AIPAC, because the facts of the issue favored him. Very importantly, too, lots of other groups in the US mobilized in support of the deal.

Some others things have also changed. Simply talking critically about AIPAC used to be rather taboo, because people were afraid of being accused of anti-Semitism or worse. That has changed a lot in recent years, partly because that accusation has been so over-used and applied to so many people for whom it is obviously not true. More people are willing to raise legitimate questions about lobby's influence, the special relationship with Israel, and Israel's policies. The result is that we are getting more accurate information and attaining more open discussion of these issues. The internet and the blogosphere are something of a game changer as well.

Moreover, the Jewish community in America has become more diverse over time. Groups like J Street, Americans for Peace Now, and Jewish Voice for Peace are offering very different views of these questions than AIPAC and its allies.

Last but not least, from day one the Obama administration made repeated and genuine efforts to advance the two-state solution, not because it was anti-Israel, but rather because it was strongly pro-

Israel and it understood that the two state-solution was the only way to guarantee Israel's long-term future. The Obama administration has gotten essentially no cooperation at all from the Netanyahu government. This is increasingly obvious to anyone who is paying attention.

But make no mistake. Despite all these reasons why the lobby is somewhat less powerful than it once was, AIPAC and the Israel lobby are still there; and on the questions of military aid, diplomatic protection— for example in the UN security council—and the peace process itself, I don't expect US policy to change very much anytime soon. I say that with some regret, I might add, because I think that the current situation is not only bad for the US and not only a genuine tragedy for the Palestinians and other people in the region, but also bad for Israel itself.

Put all these reasons together and it's hardly surprising that recent Middle East policy has been a parade of failures. What is especially striking is that it doesn't seem to matter who is in the White House. President Obama hasn't screwed up quite as dramatically as President George W. Bush did, but that's not saying much. In fact, neither Obama nor Bill Clinton did particularly well in this part of the world. Indeed, the only two presidents in recent memory who had truly successful Middle East policies were Jimmy Carter and the first President Bush, in part because they were willing to challenge the Israel lobby. It is worth noting, if you read former Israeli Foreign Minister Shlomo Ben Ami's book, that he says they both did the most for Israeli security, because they were willing to tackle Israel's more ardent supporters in the US![1]

A Shape for Future Policy

So, what should the US do instead? First, do no harm. Overactive US engagement does more harm than good, so my first recommendation is for the US to do less. The US does not know how to fix the Middle East and therefore it is foolish to try. Second, the US should return to an offshore balancing strategy. This means no large military forces in region. Keep the Rapid Deployment Force well offshore and over the horizon unless it is actually needed. The US should intervene only in extreme circumstances to preserve the balance of power, as we did in the first Gulf War. Don't do regime change, because we have no idea what to replace even bad regimes with. One of the

---

[1] Shlomo Ben Ami, *Scars of War, Wounds of Peace: The Israeli-Arab Tragedy* (New York: Oxford University Press, 2007).*

things we've learned is that one thing worse than a truly bad government is no government at all. The US should let local actors deal with issues like ISIS, which is not nearly as serious a challenge as we've been led to believe.

A corollary of all of this is that the US should have normal, business-like relations with the states of the Middle East, instead of special relationships. US strategic interests are best served by a regional balance of power and preserving that balance requires flexibility. The US should strive for cordial ties with all states in the region, instead of having special relations with some and ostracizing others. To be blunt, there are no states in the region sufficiently important or sufficiently aligned with US values and interests to warrant special relationships anymore: not Turkey, not Israel, not Egypt, not Saudi Arabia. Having businesslike relationships with everyone in the region would give Washington greater flexibility. Also, this would encourage other Middle East states to do more to retain our approval.

One thing to remember is that the US is ten thousand miles away, so we can take a more measured view of what happens there. This is not an argument for isolationism. It is an argument for strategic discipline and maybe also for occasionally playing 'hard to get' in terms of offering US support.

Last but not least, we want to build on the agreement with Iran. The US and Iran are still at odds on many issues, but now have the opportunity to explore the possibility of reversing thirty-five years of rancor and rivalry. It might not work, but we should certainly *explore* that possibility.

The Middle East is a mess. The US does not know how to fix it. Even if it did, it couldn't do it all by itself. In fact, no one can fix what is going on in the Middle East today if any major player is excluded. So we should keep talking to Iran and be open to cooperating with Iran and everyone else in the region when our interests align. I might add that this is not what most of the US foreign-policy establishment is saying today. Some people are saying—for opportunistic reasons, i.e., to look hawkish and tough—that the US now needs to get tough with Iran, which is exactly the wrong thing to do. It might even jeopardize the Iran nuclear deal itself.

There is one piece of good news in this rather bleak assessment and that is that there is great room for improvement. US Middle East policy over the past twenty years has been mostly a disaster, but that means that there is nowhere to go but up. All we need to do is stop repeating the same mistakes, learn from our past mistakes, and be open to a very different approach. In short, not only do I think the United States cannot manage the Middle East, I think it would be better for everyone if we stopped trying.

The Iran Nuclear Deal
Some Critical Questions
Noam Chomsky

George Orwell is famous for his scathing and sardonic critique of thought control under totalitarian dystopia. But less attention is paid to his discussion of how even in free societies unpopular ideas can be suppressed without the use of force, and how inconvenient facts are kept dark without the imposition of any official ban.[1] He was speaking of England, of course. He provided only a few words of explanation, but they were to the point. One pertinent comment was his observation on a quality education at the best schools, where it is instilled into you that there are certain things that "it wouldn't do to say"— or, we can add, even to think.

---

[1] See George Orwell, *Animal Farm* (New York: Signet, 1946). For a video presentation of a very similar version of this address and a similar use of Orwell's thought, see "Noam Chomsky on George Orwell, the Suppression of Ideas and the Myth of American Exceptionalism," *Democracy Now!* (Sept. 22, 2015). Available online at: www.democacynow.org/2015/9/22/noam_chomsky_on_the_myth_of (accessed 7/12/16).*

These words come to mind in considering the raging debate about the Iran nuclear deal that recently occupied center stage—a raging debate in the US, virtually alone. Almost everywhere else the agreement has been welcomed with relief and optimism and almost without even any review. This is one of many illustrations of the famous notion of "American exceptionalism."

That "America is an exceptional nation" we are informed regularly by virtually every political figure, and more interestingly, by prominent academic and public intellectuals. To select almost at random, the Professor of the Science of Government at Harvard, a distinguished liberal scholar and government adviser, instructs us in Harvard's prestigious journal *International Security* that unlike other countries, the "national identity" of the United States is "defined by a set of universal political and economic values," namely "liberty, democracy, equality, private property, and markets," so the United States has a solemn duty to maintain its "international primacy" for the benefit of the world.[1] And since this is a matter of *definition*,

---

[1] See Samuel Huntington, "Why International Primacy Matters," *International Security* 17.4 (Spring 1993): 68–83.*

we may dispense with the tedious work of empirical verification.

Or to turn to the leading left-liberal intellectual journal, the *New York Review*, the former chair of the Carnegie Endowment for International Peace observes that "American contributions to international security, global economic growth, freedom, and human well-being have been so self-evidently unique and have been so clearly directed to others' benefit that Americans have long believed that the United States amounts to a different kind of country. Where others push their national interests, the US tries to advance universal principles."[1] It is all too easy to continue.

It would be only fair to add that similar pronouncements are familiar from other imperial states in their day in the sun: Britain, France, and others. Even from very honorable figures, from whom one would have expected better. John Stuart Mill, to mention a significant case.

In some respects, American exceptionalism is not in doubt. One current example, as I mentioned, is the Iran nuclear deal, where the isolation of the United

---

[1] See Jessica T. Mathews, "The Road from Westphalia," *New York Review* (March 19, 2015). Available online at: www.nybooks.com/articles/2015/03/19/road-from-westphalia/ (accessed 7/12/16).*

States was dramatic and stark and significant. There are many other cases, but this is the one I would like to think about in this essay.

US isolation might soon increase. Throughout the process, the Republican Party tried to block the agreement. It managed to get a majority, but not enough to override a veto, so it did not quite make it. Still, the Republican Party is dedicated to undermining the deal, interestingly with the kind of unanimity that is seldom found in political parties, but could be found only in such organizations as the old Communist Party with the doctrine of democratic centralism—that everyone has to say the same thing. That is today's Republican Party—one-hundred percent unanimity on the party line. It is one indication that the Republicans are no longer a political party, despite pretensions, but rather they are a "radical insurgency" that has abandoned parliamentary politics, as they are described by the respected conservative political commentators Thomas Mann and Norman Ornstein.[1] And they may succeed in increasing sanctions, even

[1] Thomas Mann and Norman Ornstein, "Finding the Common Good in an Era of Dysfunctional Government," *Brooking Brief* (April 26, 2013). Available online at: www.brookings.edu/research/articles/2013/04/26-common-good-ysfunctional-governance-mann-ornstein (accessed 7/12/16).*

secondary sanctions, and other actions that might eventually lead Iran to opt out of the agreement with the United States.

That, however, need not mean that the agreement will be nullified. Contrary to the way it is often presented here, it is not a US-Iran agreement: rather, an agreement between Iran and P5+1, i.e., the permanent members of the UN Security Council and Germany. And the other participants might decide to proceed, as India and China have already done in part through these years in various ways, joining the large majority of the world's population, the non-aligned movement, which all along has vigorously supported Iran's right to pursue its nuclear programs. All of this deal making is, by the way, an interesting aside on Iran's alleged "isolation." Iran is isolated from the United States and whoever decides to go along with the United States, but not from the great majority of the world.

If Iran and others continue to honor the deal, the United States will be isolated from the world. This is not an unfamiliar position. That is also the background for Obama's other main foreign policy achievement, the beginning of normalization of relations with Cuba. On Cuba, the United States has been almost totally isolated for decades. Take a look at the annual votes in the United Nations General Assembly on the embargo. The only country that votes with the United States on this embargo is Israel—and Israel, itself, violates the embargo, but they have to vote with the master. In fact it was the extreme isolation from the rest of the hemisphere that finally induced Washington to acquiesce to the otherwise unanimous demand to accept Cuba within the hemispheric organizations, from which the United States would be otherwise excluded. In the United States, Obama's move was portrayed as a courageous move to end Cuba's isolation, though in reality the US's isolation was the true motivating factor. This is understood throughout the world, but not mentioned here in the US.

In the case of Iran, the reasons for US concerns, virtually alone, are clearly articulated: Iran is the greatest threat to world peace, as we hear regularly from high places, commentators and others. In the US, that is. There is also a world out there, which has its own opinions. We can easily find these out from standard sources such as Gallup polls of international opinion. One question posed is: which country is the greatest threat to world peace? The answer is unequivocal: the United States is considered to be the greatest threat to world peace, by a huge margin. No one else is even close. Far behind in second place is Pakistan. Iran is scarcely mentioned.[1]

But that is just the world. This is one of the things "it wouldn't do to say." The results found by the leading US polling agency did not make it through the portals of the free press as not the kind of thing Americans should hear.

Given the reigning American doctrine about the gravity of the Iranian threat, we can understand the virtually unanimous stand that the United States is entitled to react with force, unilaterally, if it claims to detect some Iranian departure from the terms of the agreement. Again picking an example virtually at random, consider the recent lead editorial in the *Washington Post*. It calls on Congress to "make clear that Mr. Obama or his successor will have support for immediate U.S. military action if an Iranian attempt to build a bomb is detected."[2]

---

[1] See, for example, "US is the Greatest Threat to World Peace: Poll," *Washington Post* (Jan. 5, 2014). Available online at: http://nypost.com/2014/01/05/us-is-the-greatest-threat-to-world-peace-poll/ (accessed 7/12/16).*

[2] See Editorial Board, "Next Steps on Iran," *Washington Post* (Sept. 12, 2015). Available online at: www. Washington-post.com/opinions/next-steps-on-iran/2015/09/12/e93c8c8e-58a7-11e5-abe9-27d53f250b11_story.html (accessed 7/12/16).*

The editors again make it clear that the United States is a rogue state, in the technical sense, indifferent to international law and conventions, entitled to resort to violence at will. But the editors can't be faulted for this stand, since it is almost universally assumed among the political class in this exceptional nation—though what it means is again one of those things it wouldn't do to say.

The *Washington Post* editors also make clear why the US should be prepared to take such extreme steps in its role of "international primacy." If the United States is not prepared to resort to military force, then Iran may "*escalate* its attempt to establish hegemony over the Middle East by force"—what President Obama calls repeated "Iranian aggression."[1] For those who are unaware of how Iran has been attempting to establish hegemony over the Middle East by force, or even might dream of doing so, the editors give two examples: its support for the Assad regime and for Hezbollah.

I won't insult your intelligence by commenting on this demonstration that Iran has been seeking to establish hegemony over the region by force. On Iranian "aggression," there is actually an example. I

---

[1] "Next Steps on Iran," emphasis added.*

think one example in the last couple hundred years, namely Iranian conquest of two Arab islands in the Gulf—under the regime of the Shah with strong US support.

These shocking Iranian efforts to establish regional hegemony by force may be contrasted with the actions of NATO ally Turkey in support of the Jihadi coalition in the north of Syria, support so strong that Turkey appears to have helped its allies in the al-Qaeda-affiliated al-Nusra front to kill and capture the small force introduced into Syria by the Pentagon in 2015. After several years of training and who knows how much money invested, the Pentagon managed to get fifty people into Syria, who were immediately killed or captured apparently with the help of Turkish intelligence to their allies.[1] Or more important, the central, crucial role of US ally Saudi Arabia for the Jihadi rebels in Syria and Iraq and, more generally, Saudi Arabia's having been a "major source of financing to rebel and terrorist organizations since the 1980s," in

---

[1] See, for example, Kareem Shaheen, "US-Trained Syrian Rebels Killed and Leaders Captured by al-Qaida Affiliate," *The Guardian* (July 31, 2015). Available online at: https://www.theguardian.com/world/2015/jul/31/us-trained-rebels-killed-captured-syrian-al-qaida-affiliate-nusra (accessed 7/12/16).*

the words of a study of the European Parliament. And still more generally, the missionary zeal with which Saudi Arabia promulgates its radical extremist Wahhabi-Salafi doctrines by establishing Koranic schools and mosques and dispatching radical clerics throughout the Muslim world, with enormous impact. One of the closest observers of the region, Patrick Cockburn, writes that the "Wahhabization" of mainstream Sunni Islam from Saudi Arabia is "one of the most dangerous developments of our era"— always with strong US support.[1] These are all things that it wouldn't do to mention.

All things "it wouldn't do" to mention, along with the fact that these pernicious developments are a direct outgrowth of the long-term tendency of the US, like Britain before it, to support radical Islam in opposition to secular nationalism.

Others, like UN Ambassador Samantha Power, condemn Iran's destabilization of the region. Destabilization is an interesting concept of political

---

[1] See Patrick Cockburn, "The Involvement of Salafism/ Wahhabism in the Support and Supply of Arms to Rebel Groups around the World," European Parliament Policy Department (2013). Available online at: www.europarl.europa.eu /RegData/ etudes/etudes/join/2013/457137/EXPOET_ET%282013%294571 37_EN.pdf (accessed 7/12/16).*

discourse. So, when Iran comes to the aid of the government of Iraq and Iraqi Kurdistan in defense against the attacks of ISIS, that is destabilization, if not aggression. In contrast, when the US invades Iraq, kills hundreds of thousands of people, drives millions from their homes, practically destroys the country, sets off a sectarian conflict that is now tearing Iraq and the entire region to shreds, and on the side, increases terrorism worldwide by a factor of seven in just the first year—that is called "stabilization."

The exceptionalism of US doctrinal institutions is wondrous to behold.

The *Washington Post* editors also join Obama's negotiator Dennis Ross, Thomas Friedman, and other notables in calling on Washington to provide Israel with B-52s and perhaps even the more advanced B-2 bombers and huge "bunker busters" or *Massive Ordnance Penetrators* (even though there is kind of a problem, namely Israel does not have airstrips for them).[1] None of this, of course, is for defense, but to

---

[1] For overviews of these issues, see Dennis Ross and David H. Petraeus, "How To Put Some Teeth into the Nuclear Deal with Iran," *The Washington Post* (August 25, 2015). Available online at: www.washingtonpost.com/opinions/how-to-put-some-teeth-into-the-nuclear-deal-with-iran/2015/08/25/6f3db 43c-4b35-11e5-bfb9-9736d04fc8e4_story.html; David Deptula and Michael Makovsky, "Sending a Bunker-Buster Message to

enable Israel to bomb Iran if it chooses to do so. And as a US client, it inherits from the master the freedom from international law.

The violation of international law goes far beyond threat, to action, including acts of war, which are proudly proclaimed—presumably because this is our right as an exceptional nation. One example is the very successful sabotage of Iranian installations by cyberwar, also proudly proclaimed. The Pentagon regards cyberwar as an act of war justifying a violent military response. NATO affirmed the same position a year ago, determining that aggression through cyberattacks may trigger the collective defense obligations of the NATO powers. Attacks against us, that is; not by us. The significance of these stands is, again, something that it "wouldn't do" to mention.

Perhaps the US and Israel are justified in cowering in terror before Iran because of its extraordinary military power. To evaluate this concern, we may turn to the authoritative analysis of

---

Iran," *The Wall Street Journal* (April 7, 2014). Available online at: www.wsj.com/news/articles/SB10001424052702304184045794 62970629373280; and David Axe, "Neocon Scheme: Send Nuke Bombers to Israel," *The Daily Beast* (Oct. 20, 2015). Available online at: http://www.thedailybeast.com/articles2015/10/21/neocon-scheme-send-nuke-bombers-to-israel. html (all accessed 7/12/16).*

the Center for Strategic and International Studies (CSIS) from April 2015, which finds "a conclusive case that the Arab Gulf states have… an overwhelming advantage [over] Iran in both military spending and access to modern arms."[1] For the Gulf Cooperation Council states—Bahrain, Kuwait, Oman, Saudi Arabia, and the UAE (which outspend Iran on arms by a factor of eight)—the imbalance that goes back decades. The CSIS observes further that "[t]he Arab Gulf states have acquired and are acquiring some of the most advanced and effective weapons in the world [while] Iran has essentially been forced to live in the past, often relying on systems originally delivered at the time of the Shah," which are virtually obsolete.[2] The imbalance is of course even greater with Israel, which, along with the most advanced US weaponry and its role as a virtual offshore military base of the global superpower, has a stock of nuclear weapons.

---

[1] Anthony H. Cordesman, "Military Spending and Arms Sales in the Gulf," *Center for Strategic and International Studies* (April 28 2015). Available online at: www.csis.org/analysis/ military-spending-and-arms-sales-gulf (accessed 7/12/16).*

[2] "SIPRI data also indicate that the Arab Gulf states in the GCC have a massive lead over Iran in arms imports. The gap is so great in given periods that the GCC states lead Iran by nearly 7:1 during 1997–2007, 10:1 in 2004–2008, 33:1 in 2009–2013, and 27.5:1 in 2007–2014." Cordesman, "Military Spending."*

There are, of course, other threats that justify serious concern. A nuclear weapons state might leak nuclear weapons to *jihadis*. This threat is real, but not from Iran. In the case of Iran, the threat is minuscule. Not only are the Sunni *jihadis* Iran's mortal enemies, but the ruling clerics, whatever one thinks of them, have shown no signs of clinical insanity and they know that if there was even a hint that they were the source of a leaked weapon, they and all they possess would be instantly destroyed.

That doesn't mean that we should ignore the threat, however. Not from Iran, but from US ally Pakistan, where the threat is very real. It is discussed recently by two leading Pakistani nuclear scientists, Pervez Hoodbhoy and Zia Mian, who write that increasing fears of "militants seizing nuclear weapons or materials and unleashing nuclear terrorism [have led to] the creation of a dedicated force of over 20,000 troops to guard nuclear facilities. There is no reason to assume, however, that this force would be immune to the problems associated with the units guarding regular military facilities," which have frequently suffered attacks with "insider help."[1] In other words, they are laced with *jihadi* elements all the way through, thanks to our Saudi friends and to the US itself, which has supported these activities for decades.

In brief, the problem is real enough, and is not being seriously addressed; rather, it is displaced by fantasies concocted for other reasons about an official enemy.

Opponents of the deal maintain that Iran is intent on developing nuclear weapons. Though US intelligence can discern no evidence for this, there is no doubt that in the past they have indeed intended to do so. We know this because it was clearly proclaimed. The highest authority of the Iranian state informed foreign journalists that Iran would develop nuclear weapons "certainly, and sooner than one thinks." The father of Iran's nuclear energy program and former head of Iran's Atomic Energy Organization was confident that the leadership's plan "was to build a nuclear bomb." A CIA report also had "no doubt" that

---

[1] See Pervez Hoodbhoy and Zia Mian, "Nuclear Fears, Hopes and Realities in Pakistan," *International Affairs* 90.5 (2014): *1125–1142.**

Iran would develop nuclear weapons if neighboring countries did (as they have).[1]

All of this was under the Shah, the highest authority just quoted. That is, during the period when high US officials—Dick Cheney, Donald Rumsfeld, Henry Kissinger, and others—were urging the Shah to proceed with nuclear programs, and pressuring universities to accommodate these efforts. As part of these efforts, my own university, MIT, made a deal with the Shah to admit Iranian students to the nuclear engineering program in return for grants from the Shah. This was over the very strong objections of the student body, but with comparably strong faculty support, a distinction that raises a number of interesting questions.

Opponents of the nuclear deal argue that it did not go far enough, and some supporters agree, demanding that the whole of the Middle East rid itself of weapons of mass destruction. I am quoting Iran's Minister of Foreign Affairs, Javad Zarif, reiterating the call of the nonaligned movement and the Arab States

---

[1] On Iran's historic claims regarding nuclear ambitions and US assessments of those claims, see, for example, Gary Samore, ed., *Iran's Strategic Weapons Programmes: A Net Assessment* (International Institute for Strategic Studies; New York: Routledge, 2005).*

for many years to establish a Weapons of Mass Destruction zone—WMD-free zone in the Middle East.[1]

That would be a straightforward way to address whatever threat Iran is alleged to pose. But still more is at stake. Two of the leading figures in the international antinuclear movement, veterans of Pugwash and UN agencies, write in *Arms Control Today* that "[t]he successful adoption in 1995 of the resolution on the establishment of a zone free of weapons of mass destruction (WMD) in the Middle East was the main element of a package that permitted the indefinite extension of the [Non-Proliferation Treaty]."[2] Hence perpetuation of the most important arms-control treaty is threatened by failure to move towards a WMD-free zone in the Middle East. Repeatedly, implementation of this plan has been blocked by the US at the five-year review meetings of

---

[1] See Javad Zarif, "Iran Has Signed a Historic Nuclear Deal—Now It's Israel's Turn," *Iran Review* (July 31, 2015). Available online at: http://www.iranreview.org/content/ Documents/Iran-Has-Signed-A-Historic-Nuclear-Deal-Now-It-s-Israel-s-Turn.htm (accessed 7/12/16).*

[2] Jayantha Dhanapala and Sergio Duarte, "Is There a Future for the NPT?" *Arms Control Today* (July/August 2015). Available online at: www.armscontrol.org/ACT/2015_0708 /Features/Is-There-a-Future-for-the-NPT (accessed 7/12/16).*

the Non-Proliferation Treaty, most recently by Obama in 2010 and again in 2015.

The same two antinuclear specialists comment that in 2015 the effort was again blocked "on behalf of a state that is not a party to the NPT and is widely believed to be the only one in the region possessing nuclear weapons," a polite and understated reference to Israel. Washington's sabotage of the possibility in defense of Israel's nuclear weapons systems may well undermine the NPT as well as "stabilize" the Middle East by maintaining dangerous instability. This is, incidentally, not the only case when opportunities to end the alleged Iranian threat have been undermined by Washington, raising further questions about just what is actually at stake.[1]

Turning to that, what actually is the threat posed by Iran? Plainly it is not a military threat. We can put aside the fevered pronouncements about Iranian aggression, support for terror, and seeking hegemony by force, or the still more outlandish notion that even if Iran had a bomb it might use it, therefore suffering instant obliteration.

The real threat has been clearly explained by US intelligence, which informed Congress that "Iran's

---

[1] Dhanapala and Duarte, "Is There a Future?"*

nuclear program and its willingness to keep open the possibility of developing nuclear weapons is a central part of its deterrent strategy."[1] That Iran has a serious interest in a deterrent strategy is hardly in doubt among serious analysts and is recognized by US intelligence. The influential analyst and CIA veteran Bruce Riedel, himself no dove, observes that "If I was an Iranian national security planner, I would want nuclear weapons" as a deterrent. He also points out that Israel's "strategic room for maneuver in the region would be constrained by an Iranian nuclear deterrent."[2] That also holds true for the United States.

For the two rogue states that rampage freely in the region, any deterrent is unacceptable, and for those accustomed to rule by force that concern is easily escalated to an "existential threat." That I think is the heart of the matter—even if it wouldn't do to say, or to think.

---

[1] John J. Kruzel, "Report to Congress Outlines Iranian Threats," *DoD News* (April 10, 2010). Available online at: http://archive.defense.gov/news/newsarticle.aspx?id=58833 (accessed 7/12/16).*

[2] See Scott Peterson, "What Would Happen if Iran Had the Bomb?" *Christian Science Monitor* (Feb. 16, 2012). Available online at: http://www.csmonitor.com/World/Middle-East/2012/0216/What-would-happen-if-Iran-had-the-bomb-video (accessed 7/12/16).*

Peacemaking as a Journey of Transformation
Our Inner Strength & Public Engagement

Jean Zaru

Sisters and brothers, I have traveled here today to share with you my personal witness to peacemaking in my native land of Palestine, where to be actively engaged in building a culture of peace and nonviolence means to do so in a context of severe oppression, military occupation, and continued displacement.

Friends, I come to you representing a narrative of exclusion—the denial of basic human and community rights of my people. From the heart of Palestine I have come, from the midst of an indigenous people, from a nation held in captivity.

Sixty-seven years ago we were cast aside from the course of history, our very identity denied, our human, cultural, and historical reality suppressed. We became victims of an exclusivist agenda that usurped our rights, our land, and our water and confiscated our historical narrative, as well. We became victims of a colonialist program.

More than 500 villages were either depopulated or destroyed in what became Israel, leaving hundreds of thousands of Palestinians either as refugees or internally displaced persons. Today, Palestinians constitute the largest and the longest-standing single refugee population in the world. Over five million of us are waiting to return home. Those who remained in what later became the State of Israel continue to experience exclusion and discrimination in their historical homeland. And those of us who, in 1967, came under Israeli occupation in the West Bank, the Gaza Strip, and East Jerusalem have since been subjected to a unique combination of military occupation, settler colonization and systematic oppression.

I have lived all my life in Ramallah, and more than half of my life under Israeli occupation, but it was never as difficult as it is today. "Normal life" for Palestinians living in the occupied territories has disappeared. We are subjected to a policy of restrictions on our movement; a policy of intentional impoverishment, imprisonment, and house demolitions; the illegal confiscation of our land and water resources; and the destruction of our crops and thousands of our trees. More than eighty percent of our water in the West Bank is siphoned off; sometimes sold back to us, but at very high prices. So, you see, we are not only dealing with direct violence, but with structural violence that is political, economic, cultural, religious, and environmental.

There is, indeed, an endless battering of Palestinians on a daily basis that either imprisons us in our own homes or leaves us to live within fragmented communities separated from each other by endless walls, ditches, and checkpoints, making the means of daily life—jobs, trade, education, health care—all but inaccessible. The people, land, houses, and trees have been brutally treated. Fear and insecurity are rapidly replacing compassion and trust.

Relations have become hard and tense. For when almost every aspect of life is framed in oppression and humiliation, moral space is diminished. Our own humanity is threatened and role models for our children become hard to find. People are tired and depressed. They are traumatized by the violence that is perpetuated against them, which affects both their physical and mental health.

And yet, despite all of this I also come with a message of hope! It is a message of hope embodied in the spirit and will of all those throughout the world who refuse to submit to forces of oppression, who refuse to submit to violence, injustice, and structures of domination.

Indeed, hope is revealed when truth is spoken. It is within this light that I share with you that the most basic form of deception in my context is the fabrication of a fake symmetry between occupier and occupied, between oppressor and victim. For me it is clear: the Israeli military occupation of the West Bank, Gaza Strip, and East Jerusalem must end. It is illegal according to international law and furthermore, the occupation entails the most pervasive forms of violence, the most direct denials of human rights violations, and the completely immoral enslavement of an entire nation. It is the ultimate provocation at both the individual and collective level.

Nevertheless, no degree of violence, whether direct or structural, can succeed in subjugating the will of a people or destroying their spirit when they are struggling for their freedom, dignity, and right to sovereignty on their own land. All attempts at intensifying the brutality of the occupation have only led to the escalation of the conflict and increased our determination to gain our liberty.

Conflicts can only be resolved politically and legally, on the basis of parity of rights and the global rule of law. All peoples, without double standards, should adhere to United Nations Security Council resolutions and international law, including the Geneva Conventions. No state is above the law.

It is important to remind ourselves that the victims of oppression are not always blameless. For, too often, they themselves become the oppressors of others. They seem to forget that the humanity of the oppressor is violated at the very moment of oppressing another human being. Hence, the *liberation of the oppressed and violated will also lead to the liberation of the oppressor.*

Jesus distilled from the long experience of his people that nonviolent resistance was a way of opposing evil without becoming evil in the process. He advocated for means that were consistent with the desired end, that is: a society of justice, peace, and equality. He repeatedly spoke of the reign of God that is free of domination. We pray constantly for God's will on earth as it is in heaven. In other words, we are calling for the reign of God.

But how do we move beyond word to actualizing that reign? This is our challenge together.

WHERE is God's reign?

God's reign is wherever domination is overcome, wherever people are freed, wherever the soul is fed, wherever God's reality is known.

WHEN is God's reign?

God's reign is whenever people turn away from worshiping power, wealth, and fame. It is whenever we insist on creating a society of equals.

WHAT is God's reign?

God's reign is the transformation of the **Domination System** into a nonviolent, humane, ecologically sustainable, livable environment that enables all creation to grow and live well.

The reign of God cannot just be inner or outer; it must be both or it is neither.

When I received the invitation to speak at this conference, for a moment I was excited about the possibility to be with all of you. But then, remembering my last trip to Jordan (for I, as a West Bank Palestinian, am not allowed to fly out of the Tel Aviv airport), my heart sank.

It should take less than one hour to travel from Ramallah to the one bridge that West Bank Palestinians are permitted to use to exit our country. However, when I crossed two months ago, it took five to six hours to cross the border itself and subsequently arrive in Amman even in an ambulance, for I was very sick. The tolls are many. And even if I take this one small example of crossing the bridge, it is difficult to fully describe. For the tolls involved in traveling under occupation drain our lives, impair our health, add to our financial burden, and increase our separation anxieties, as neither leaving nor returning is ever guaranteed. The State of Israel has claimed that these measures are for security. And so I wonder whether they can, with all their sophisticated devices, check our hearts and minds as well. Can they see how we feel? Do they notice our pain? Or is this not part of the security check? Or not part of building peace with one's neighbor?

So often I feel like screaming: "We are sacred! We are part of God's creation! Why do you treat us like this?" And other times I feel like crying out the words of the Psalmist:

My God, my God why have you forsaken me?
Why are you so far from helping me,
from the words of my groaning?
Oh my God, I cry by day,
But you do not answer;
And by night, but find no rest. Psalm 22:1–2

As I look at the people around me during the long waiting hours at the checkpoints or in the bus to cross the bridge, I listen to their conversations and I hear individual stories of pain, of families being torn apart, of despair and suffering, of longing and fear. Yet, hope is strengthened when I see the sharing of food and water, the compassionate offers to help the elderly and young mothers with children. Hope is strengthened when we see the divine quality in those with whom we differ and, yes, even the divine quality in those who impose the persecution!

Without a doubt, the way of transformation calls us to stand against the forces of death and evil, both within us and around us. It challenges us to resist the temptation simply to re-arrange the furniture, whether that re-arrangement is in the structures of our psyche or those of our planet.

What is that inner force that drives us, that provides regeneration and perseverance to speak the truth that so desperately needs to be spoken in this moment in history? I am older, my health poor, my body fragile, and yet, as do so many others, I believe that I have no choice but to bear witness to what is happening in my land, to expose the structures of violence and domination, to bring them out into the light, and thereby undercut their power. If I deserve credit for courage, it is not for anything I do here, but for continuing in my daily struggle under occupation on so many fronts, for remaining *samida* (steadfast) and, all the while, remaining open to love, to the beauty of the earth, and contributing to its healing when it is violated.

My friends, struggle changes us in profound ways.

For the essence of struggle is neither endurance nor is it denial. Rather, the essence of struggle is the decision to become new rather than simply to become older. That is, within the essence of struggle lies the opportunity to grow either smaller or larger, to become more than what we already are or to retreat into becoming less. Indeed, the process of life itself may be found within this opportunity.

For life is about movement. And every day we either become more or we diminish.

In the struggle, and in this particular struggle, we cannot give up.

In so many ways, struggle gives life depth and vision, insight and understanding, compassion and character. It not only transforms us, but empowers us to be a TRANSFORMING PEOPLE, as well.

It is vitally important that we insist on a prophetic ministry in today's threatened world, one that exposes the lies and myths that have been created, mainly by the powerful, to cover up the pain and grief of our world. This prophetic ministry should resist the monopoly of knowledge and the power. Rather, it should struggle to forge a new discourse, one that includes critique from the margins. Therefore, it is essential that all engaged in such a ministry make contact in each and every place with the refugees, the displaced, the political prisoners, and the downtrodden. Spaces must be created for such people to share their stories of grief, as well as to express their anger and hope.

Those who engage in prophetic renewal are called to be Truth Tellers, rather than people who remain silent or re-route the conversation. Contemporary culture is marked by the great cover-up. And this is certainly true in the case of Palestine. One of the most important tasks before us as peacemakers is to educate ourselves to be effective speakers, writers, teachers, and preachers, so that our silence is no more and our voice is informed.

This task is especially important, for half-truths and lies fill government halls, institutions, and the media, reminding one of the lament of the prophet Jeremiah,

They all deceived their neighbors and nobody speaks the truth;

They have taught their tongues to speak lies.
Jeremiah 9:5

These are very hard days in Palestine. The settlement expansion and the construction of the Wall continue unabated. International law and UN resolutions sit collecting dust. While the political landscape has changed dramatically in recent weeks, months, and years, and global powers maneuver a response, humanitarian aid is used like a playing card without regard to ordinary families struggling to secure their daily bread.

My friends, we have been working for a long time to end oppression and occupation and have, thus far, not secured our rights. It is discouraging. Fear and loss surround us, and many forces are at work to make us feel marginalized and disempowered. At best the work ahead seems overwhelming.

What do we do?

What actions do we take?

Some of my people have opted to withdraw, that is to either withdraw internally or to both leave Palestine and withdraw internally. In fact, many have responded in this manner because they truly perceive their situation as intolerable. Regardless of the motivation, withdrawal cushions us from feeling the full impact of our situation, and it also cuts us off from information and observations vital to our survival as a people. When we withdraw, our gifts and our perceptions often get buried. The realities of domination go unchallenged, leading to neither inner nor outer transformation.

Other people have chosen to accommodate, comply, or manipulate. When we manipulate, we have the illusion of being in control. We can reap some rewards, but in doing so we are accepting the system's terms, its unspoken rules and values, including the often negative values it accords to us. Furthermore, manipulation does not challenge the low value the system places on individuals. In order to manipulate, we cannot be ourselves, express our true feelings, or share our real perceptions; we literally mask ourselves. Manipulation may get us some of the system's rewards, but it neither liberates us individually nor transforms the structures of domination.

The alternative is to RESIST. Resistance challenges the system's values and categories. Resistance speaks its own truth to power, and shifts the ground of struggle to its own terrain.

Resistance is often thought of as negative. However, resistance is the refusal to be neglected. Today, Palestinians find themselves embedded in structures that neglect their humanity and human rights; only acts of resistance can transform these structures. And I, along with many others, have opted for the path of active nonviolent resistance. To resist is to be human, and yet resistance is not easy. It requires constant, hard work. Indeed, it is not easy to sustain the path of nonviolent resistance for years and years, over many issues. None of us can resist all the time, in every area of life. We must choose our battles, meaning we must choose the priorities of struggle.

But the question remains: where do we find sustenance? How are we re-energized, how are we empowered to continue to go forward on the path of resisting structures of domination and establishing the reign of God, indeed establishing a household of life?

I believe that we continue because something is so sacred to us, so sacred that it means more than our comfort and convenience. It might be God, or the Spirit, or the sacredness of life, or Mother Earth, or equality and freedom, or human rights and human dignity. Whatever it is and whatever we call it, it CAN nurture us. To be nurtured personally empowers and sustains us as individuals. But in the struggle we need community. We need each other and we need to build together a local and global movement for peace with justice, for the struggle is one.

As a peace and solidarity movement, we have been accused of lacking a clear vision regarding the kind of future we want. I think we do have a vision, which includes diversity and pluralism, and rejects uniform dogmatic, exclusive formulations. We want a world of freedom and justice for all. In order to attain this, we need to mobilize people, but not around fear, anger, or blame, nor out of guilt and shame. I believe that this is the moment to reinvent our strategies and our tactics to affirm and engage the possibility of moving people to act from hope and to act in the service of what they love. To create the world we want, we have to translate that hope and love into action; for faith without action is dead and useless.

I have found that times of grief and anguish can actually strengthen our bonds. And now, in such times in this movement in Palestine and Israel and beyond, we need each other as never before. We need to treat each other well, to cherish and care for and support each other to become the community we imagine. Our solidarity must go deeper than we've ever known before. Solidarity means strengthening our openness and communication with each other, our willingness to bring everyone to the table, our practice of direct democracy, as well as our commitment to build broad-based alliances and network with like-minded people.

It is now more necessary than ever to move from statements to direct nonviolent action, like divesting from structures that enable the Occupation.

Such action gives hope to the people in the forefront of the struggle. To vocally advocate for the implementation of international law and the protection of human rights gives hope, as well.

But the ugly fact remains that Palestinians have always been viewed as "a problem" for the Zionist project, whether we were good or bad, violent or non-violent. Thus far, the so-called peace process and initiatives have only proposed to minimize, not resolve the conflict that can, of course, only be accomplished by addressing the root injustices. Official Israeli policy has always been neither to accept the Palestinian people as equals nor to admit that their fundamental rights have been violated all along. Although a few courageous Israelis over the years have tried to deal with this other side of concealed history, most Israelis have made every effort to deny, avoid, or negate the Palestinian reality. This is, fundamentally, why there is no peace today.

The essence of the Israeli government position contradicts itself. While the Jewish state publicly claims that it wants peace and security, it continues to create facts on the ground that guarantee neither one nor the other. And the United States government's virtually unconditional support to Israel coupled with the political support of right-wing Christians does not make it easier. It is shocking to me that the Israeli government accepts and even welcomes the support of Christian Zionist groups who are pro-Israel politically and anti-Jewish theologically. Their theology must be rejected by all, because it is a violent, exclusive agenda that has no respect for any other group that differs with it. They demonize Islam, do not respect Judaism, and tell me as a Palestinian Christian, I am not among the chosen, but among the cursed for I stand in the way of the fulfillment of the prophecy of God.

As a Palestinian Quaker woman in the holy land, I have spent all my life confronting structures of injustice. These structures have been at work in a DEstructive way throughout our community and have caused both spiritual and physical suffering for many, including myself. I often come back to the same thought and wonder if there really is a presence of God or the indwelling divinity in every person, why is there so much evil in the world? Why is it sometimes so hard for us to see God in others?

My inward struggle has heightened my awareness of global suffering, which is, in turn, surely a reflection of the evils plaguing the human race. It has also opened me to God's redeeming love and activity.

Clearly, involvement in any just action has a price. Therefore, the question then becomes, "Am I ready to pay the price and share the suffering of others?" Suffering for me is bearable, if it is for the cause of liberation. For we not only move closer to liberation but within the very process itself we may find a new, beloved community with others and with God.

I now understand that those who operate the structures of oppression are dependent upon the people they oppress and are equally in need of liberation and God's grace. Yet, it seems to me that most often the will and strength to end the oppression comes primarily from those who bear the oppression in their own lives and those who understand their livelihood to be intertwined and thus have made the commitment to accompany them in solidarity.

We are called to conversion, to be converted to the struggle of women and men everywhere who have no way to escape the unending fatigue of their labor and the daily denial of their human rights and human worth. We must let our hearts be moved by the anguish and suffering of our sisters and brothers in Palestine, in Iraq, and throughout the world. But how can we bear the pain, and where do we look for hope? Is there anything meaningful we can do to solve the political chaos and crisis in the world? Is there anything significant we can do to stop wars of all kinds?

Let us take a look into ourselves. The outward situation is merely an expression of the inward state. It requires great self-denial and resignation of ourselves to God to be committed to peace and to nonviolent action to bring about change. This technique may seemingly have no immediate positive effect, and it may indeed lead to outward defeat. Whether successful or not it will surely involve sacrifice of some kind. However, if we believe in nonviolence as the true way of peace and love, we must make nonviolence a principle not only for individuals but also a foundation of national and universal conduct.

We should always try to avoid feeling morally superior, because we know how soon we may stumble when we are put to the test. We may talk about peace, but if we are not transformed inwardly, if we still are motivated by greed or pride, if we are nationalistic, if we are bound by beliefs and dogmas for which we are willing to destroy others, there is no way we can have peace in this world.

We, Palestinians, have gone through circumstances of great privation, anxiety, and suffering. All these seemed at times to weaken my dependence on God, but what joy and hope I gain when I know, wherever I am, whether in affluent circumstances or in poverty, whether I have personal liberty or not, that I am under the guiding hand of God and that God has a service for me to render wherever I am.

I see things differently now. I know that the oppressor is not freer than the oppressed. Both live in fear and do not have peace. Others cannot bring it to us. What will bring us peace is transformation at all levels—a transformation that leads to action. Our miseries are not going to stop because we disapprove. My misery will not stop simply because you or I disapprove. Rather, we must take action to bring about transformation of ourselves and the structures of domination.

Our shrinking world makes us all neighbors and I am increasingly aware of two facts about ourselves as inhabitants of this world. One is that we are very different from one another in color, lifestyle, culture, and belief. The other is that we are exceedingly alike. There is a fantastic range of common needs and desires, fears and hopes that bind us together in our humanness, and the well-being of each is interrelated with the well-being of all.

Through the ages people have engaged in a search for ultimate meaning in life, but they have turned this search into a political conflict, into wars and death in order to secure the dominance of a particular ideology, religion, or nation. Our age of unparalleled advancement in education, science, and technology has also been an age of enormous violence.

Meanwhile, the need for imaginative understanding, simple trust, and creative cooperation was never more urgent. Maybe the time has come when we should unite in certain common affirmations of life.

I offer the following:

1. We affirm that all forms of human power and authority are subject to God and accountable to people. This means the right to full participation in resisting oppression, the Occupation, and more generally those powers and authorities that prohibit the processes of transformation towards justice, peace, and the integrity of creation.

2. We affirm God's preferential option for the poor and oppressed. It is our duty to embrace God's action in the struggles of the poor and for the liberation of all.

3. We affirm the equal value of all races, religions, and peoples. All people reflect the rich plurality of God's creation.

4. We affirm that male and female are created in the image of God, and that we should resist

structures of patriarchy that perpetuate violence against women.

5. We affirm that truth is the foundation of freedom. We should seek to communicate the truth in imaginative, prophetic, liberating, and respectful ways.

6. We affirm that the only possible peace is one based in justice. True peace means that every human being dwells in secure relatedness to God, neighbor, nature, and self.

"The effect of righteousness will be peace, and the result of righteousness, quietness and trust forever" (Isaiah 32:17).

7. We affirm that the land belongs to God. Human use of land and waters should release the earth to replenish its life-giving power, protecting its integrity and providing ample space for its creatures. We should resist the dumping of toxic wastes into the lands and waters.

8. We affirm that there is an inseparable relationship between justice and human rights. But it must be clearly understood that we refer not only to individual rights, but also to the collective social, economic, and cultural rights of peoples. We will resist systems that violate human rights and deny the realization of the full potential of individuals and

peoples. We will resist, in particular, torture, disappearances, and extra-judicial killings.

9. We affirm the presence of a spirit of hope and compassion available to all by which our lives may be more whole, more creative, more harmonious as we draw directly upon that power around us and within us and within all life.

I have learned that the struggle for justice is one struggle, and that an action taken to subvert violence and strengthen human rights in one area is an action on behalf of people everywhere. Martin Luther King reminded us that, "injustice anywhere is a threat to justice everywhere."[1]

I now understand even more than before that our global responsibilities and relationships have a local face, and no matter where we live, we can work for human rights and a culture of peace. The kinships we form as we do so serve as a prototype for a new community, one that knows no boundaries and values interdependence.

Those of us committed to peace and justice, whether with respect to the Palestinian experience or

---

[1] Martin Luther King, Jr., "Letter from a Birmingham Jail." Available online at: https://kinginstitute.stanford.edu/king-papers/documents/letter-birmingham-jail (accessed 8/1/16).*

to any other issue, should not give up, for to give up is to give in and allow injustice to prevail. Rather, we must continue to fan the embers into flames of light; no matter how small they are, because these embers of light give hope to those in the forefront of struggle. And they will keep the work for justice and peace in the Middle East alive.

Mainstream Christian Zionism

Peter J. Miano

Zionism and its impact on contemporary Israel and Palestine are topics of enormous import and therefore demand careful examination, yet they are widely misunderstood. Zionism is often regarded as a Jewish movement. In fact, the vast majority of Zionists are Christian. Moreover, *Christian Zionism* is usually considered to be a subset of Zionism. In contrast to this popular misconception, we should understand that Christian Zionism is the majority expression of Zionism; Jewish Zionism is an outgrowth of Christian Zionism. While many consider Christian Zionism to be a phenomenon of the religious right, most Christian Zionists are mainstream, liberal Christians. For example, Reinhold Niebuhr, the iconic twentieth-century American liberal theologian, was self-consciously and consistently Zionist throughout his career.

Christian Zionism is generally associated with Christians from the "Christian right," who are loosely labeled fundamentalists or evangelicals. Sometimes, Christian Zionists are referred to as "the lunatic fringe." Understood narrowly, Christian Zionists see the establishment of the State of Israel as a necessary step in God's plan of salvation history. This is the best known form of Christian Zionism. This Christian form attracts the most critical attention, especially from mainstream Christians. However, it represents a distinct minority of Christian Zionists. The popular preoccupation with this select band on the Christian Zionist spectrum ignores the vast majority of Christian Zionists. I will refer to this strain of Zionism as *fundamentalist* or *narrow* Christian Zionism. In contrast to this narrow view, Christian Zionism, properly understood, covers a much broader range of Christians.

As a phenomenon, Christian Zionism is older than Jewish Zionism.[1] In 1621, Sir Henry Finch wrote a discourse calling for support for the Jewish people and

---

[1] The most thorough examination of fundamentalist Christian Zionism is by Stephen Sizer, *Christian Zionism: Road Map to Armageddon?* (Downers Grove, IL: IVP Academic, 2006).*

for their return to their biblical homeland.[1] Further development of its primordial form dates to the first quarter of the nineteenth-century in England and in the United States. In the nineteenth century, Christian Zionism was, indeed, a fundamentalist ideology, but it has spread far beyond the narrow boundaries of evangelicals and biblical literalists. Over the past twenty years, Christian Zionism has attracted more and more scholarly attention, but that attention has been focused almost exclusively on this select band of the fundamentalist Christian Zionist spectrum, leaving wider and more conspicuous bands of the spectrum almost totally ignored—hiding in plain sight. This preoccupation of mainstream Christians with fundamentalist Christian Zionism is both misguided and misleading. Zionism is far more pervasive among "mainstream" Christians than it is usually regarded to

---

[1] Sir Henry Finch, *The World's Resurrection or The Calling of the Jewes: A Present to Judah and the Children of Israel that Ioyned with Him, and to Ioseph (that valiant tribe of Ephraim) and all the House of Israel that Ioyned with Him* (London: Edward Griffin for William Bladen, 1621). In addition to Sizer, *Christian Zionism*, see Douglas Joel Culver, "The Contribution of Sir Henry Finch (1558–1625) to British Nonconformist Eschatology: A Study in the Organic Character and Significance of the Doctrine of National Jewish Restoration to Palestine in the Historical Context of Time" (Th.M. thesis, Trinity Evangelical Divinity School, 1973).*

be. Christian Zionism is not usually associated with mainstream, progressive Christians. This error needs to be corrected.

Christian attention to the phenomenon of Zionism is appropriate, because, paradoxically, Zionism originated as a Christian phenomenon and continues to be overwhelmingly Christian. How do I arrive at this conclusion?

Estimates of the number and percentages of fundamentalist and/or evangelical Christians in America vary depending on how one defines these terms, but most surveys estimate that about twenty-three to twenty-seven percent of the US Christian population is evangelical.[1] In 2014, for example, a Pew Research poll of 35,000 Americans put the Christian population of America at seventy percent (210 million Americans). It found that evangelical Christians make up about one quarter of the Christian population (52.5 million Americans).[2]

---

[1] According to a 2012 Gallup poll, 77% of Americans identify as Christians (231 million Americans). Available online at: www.gallup.com/poll/159548/identify-christian.aspx (accessed 3/21/16).*

[2] "America's Changing Religious Landscape," Pew Research Center (May 12, 2015). Available online at: www.pewforum.org/2015/05/12/americas-changing-religious-landscape/ (accessed 3/21/16).*

By way of contrast, consider that the world's Jewish population is about 14 million people, i.e., about one quarter of the population of evangelical American Christians. At the risk of oversimplification, but to help demonstrate my point, consider that if all Jews in the world are Zionist, but only half the evangelicals in the USA are Zionist, then American fundamentalist Christian Zionists would outnumber all Jewish Zionists in the world by about 2:1. Thus, even if all Jews in the world are Zionists—and we know this is not correct—and only half of evangelicals in the US are Zionists, then Zionism is an overwhelmingly Christian phenomenon. The ratio of American fundamentalist Christian Zionists to *American* Jewish Zionists is closer to 5:1. Once Christian Zionism is properly understood to include many progressive Christians as well, we will see that for every Jewish Zionist, there are at least ten Christian Zionists.[1]

The significance of this point should not be ignored, because Zionist apologists often advance the erroneous and specious complaint that criticism of Zionism is a new and evolved form of anti-Semitism.[2]

---

[1] I will argue below that the actual proportion is actually much greater.

[2] Paul Merkley, *Christian Attitudes towards the State of Israel* (Montreal: McGill-Queen's University Press, 2007), 4.

Zionism, however, should not be overly identified with Jews and Judaism for a number of reasons, most importantly because Christian Zionists vastly outnumber Jewish Zionists, especially once Christian Zionism is properly understood. Since Zionism has had enormous and far-reaching consequences on a national and global level and because it is overwhelmingly Christian, the examination of Christian Zionism by Christians of all persuasions is an important historical and ethical enterprise. What is more, since Zionism has produced catastrophic consequences for many people, Jews as well as non-Jews, Christian examination of Zionism, especially in its Christian forms, is a moral obligation as well. In any event, Christian examination of Christian Zionism is first and foremost an examination of Christians, Christian ideology, and Christian ethics.

My own consideration of Christian Zionism dates to the mid-1990s, when I was first introduced to it in its fundamentalist form. It was about that time that the phrase *Christian Zionism* was coined. My first essay on the subject—and I believe the first time the phrase *mainstream* Christian Zionism was employed and examined—was published in Michael Prior's last book in 2004.[1] By that time, Christian Zionism had gained considerable media attention, including a thirty-minute segment of *60 Minutes* in 2003 and feature articles in the *Washington Post* and *USA Today*. However, those segments focused on what we should consider to be only a subset of Christian Zionism (i.e., the fundamentalist version represented by John Hagee, Hal Lindsay, and the International Christian Embassy in Jerusalem). It is also illustrated in the popular *Left Behind* series of fiction books.[2] Critics frequently refer to this subset pejoratively as a Christian heresy or as the "lunatic ravings" of the Christian right.[3]

---

[1] Peter Miano, "Mainstream Christian Zionism," *Speaking the Truth: Zionism, Israel and Occupation* (ed. Michael Prior; London: Melisende, 2004), 126–47.*

[2] Tim LaHaye and Jerry B. Jenkins, *Left Behind* (Carol Stream, IL: Tyndale House Publishers, 1995). This volume has been a perpetual bestseller since its appearance, eventually spawning 11 sequels and 4 prequels, as well as scores of related product lines. According to the author's website, the original novel has sold over 63,000,000 copies. See www.leftbehind.com/01_products/browse.asp?section=Books (accessed 3/21/16).*

[3] "Apocalypse Soon: Evangelicals in the US Believe There Is a Biblical Basis for Opposing The Middle East Road Map," 10 June 2003. Available online at: www.axisoflogic.com/artman/publish/Article_517.shtml (accessed 3/21/16).*

Stephen Sizer, an English Episcopalian priest, wrote his doctoral dissertation on Christian Zionism. The dissertation is exclusively preoccupied with evangelical, fundamentalist Christian Zionism, ignoring the dominant mainstream variety, and he continues to focus his critique of Christian Zionism on this subset.[1] In 2012, Steven Paas published *Christian Zionism Examined.*[2] It focused exclusively on the fundamentalist form. In 2013, Paul Louis Metzger posted at *Patheos* a critique of Christian Zionism that focused exclusively on the fundamentalist Christian version.[3] In 2014, at a conference on Christians in the holy land, sponsored by the United Methodist General Board of Global Ministries in Ginghamsburg, Ohio, Alex Awad, a Palestinian American Baptist minister, lectured on Christian Zionism. He focused exclusively on its fundamentalist form. David Wildman, also with the

---

[1] See Stephen Sizer, *Challenging Christian Zionism: Theology, Politics and the Israel-Palestine Conflict* (London: Melisende, 2005).*

[2] Steven Paas, *Christian Zionism Examined: a Review of Ideas on Israel, the Church and the Kingdom* (Nuremberg: VTR Publications, 2012).*

[3] Paul Louis Metzger, "Zionism: Is it Biblical?" (March 5, 2013). Available online at: http://www.patheos.com/blogs/uncommongodcommongood/2013/03/christian-zionism-is-it-biblical/ (accessed 5/9/16).*

United Methodist General Board of Global Ministries, held forth frequently on the topic of Christian Zionism, always in its narrow form.[1]

Fundamentalist Christian Zionism
An Easy Target for Liberals

It is not surprising that most contemporary attention focuses on *fundamentalist* Christian Zionism. Fundamentalist Christian Zionists are vocal and visible, and therefore easily identified. Due to their distinctive and sometimes bizarre biblical interpretations, they are also easily critiqued. Recent popular and scholarly assessments of fundamentalist Christian Zionism are not wrong, but they are misleading. The problem is that defining Christian Zionism as a form of biblical literalism is a mistake. If biblical literalism defines Zionism, then most Jewish Zionists, including the foundational Jewish Zionists, like Theodore Herzl, would not qualify.

That Christian Zionism does not require a fundamentalist reading of the Bible is well recognized by fundamentalist Christian Zionists. The Rev. Malcom

---

[1] For the flavor of oral comments, see www.umcmission. org/learn-about-us/news-and-stories/2014/september/0922 erodinginjustice (accessed 3/21/16).*

Hedding, a spokesperson for the International Christian Embassy in Jerusalem, writes:

> If Zionism is the belief in the Jewish people's right to return to their homeland, then a Christian Zionist should simply be defined as a Christian who supports the Jewish people's right to return to their homeland. Under this broad and simple definition, many Christians would qualify no matter what their reasons are for this support. [1]

Understood more broadly and more correctly, the ranks of Christian Zionists include renowned mainstream Christians such as Reinhold Niehbur, Krister Stendahl, Robert Drinan, William Albright, and W. D. Davies. Public figures including John Kerry, Hillary Clinton, and the journalist James Carroll must be included among Christian Zionists. None of these are biblical literalists. All of them are Zionists. Further, almost the entire biblical academy is, if not self-consciously and directly in the service of the Zionist agenda, then at least indirectly engaged in promoting the Zionist narrative. The same can be said for mainstream churches that promote and reinforce the

---

[1] Malcom Hedding, *Christian Zionism 101: Giving Definition to the Movement.* See us.icej.org/media/christian-zionism-101 (accessed 3/21/16).*

Zionist narrative in their Sunday school curricula, hymnody, and liturgies. Finally, almost all so-called Christian-Jewish dialogue is dominated by sympathy for the Zionist agenda. Indeed, most forms of so-called Christian-Jewish dialogue exclude any consideration of the effects of the Zionist agenda on the peoples of Palestine. Mainstream Christian Zionists are progressive and liberal. They often do not declare their Zionist orientation. Their affinity for Zionism is often masked by a sincere and notable concern to correct past wrongs by Christians against Jews. They usually do not endorse the extreme policies of the State of Israel against the Palestinians in the West Bank and Gaza, although their sensitivity toward Palestinians does not usually include the Palestinian experience in 1948. One might reasonably wonder how Christians can reject on moral grounds the occupation of the West Bank and Gaza in 1967 and its aftermath, but at the same time accept the occupation of Palestine in 1948, which was far more devastating to Palestinians without any moral compunctions whatsoever?

What Then Defines Zionism and How Do We Recognize That It Is Mainstream Christians?

If Zionism does not require biblical literalism in either its Jewish or Christian forms, then what defines a Zionist and Zionism? Zionism is a nationalist movement bearing a family resemblance to all other nationalist movements of the twentieth and early twenty-first centuries and containing its own idiosyncrasies. Like any nationalist movement, it is subject to critique and it is subject to the same critique to which all nationalist movements must submit. All nationalism is exclusive. All exclusivity is divisive. All divisiveness is unstable. In my opinion, to be clear and in the interests of full disclosure, all nationalism is perverse and anachronistic. The advent of the nation-state is a modern phenomenon that has resulted in unprecedented ethnic conflict and unspeakable and unparalleled violence by peoples against each other. Zionist nationalism is no more violent than, for example, American nationalism, and no less violent, either. While they are different currently, neither is exceptional in that way. It is important to note, however, that people are sympathetic to Zionist nationalism because first they are sympathetic to the concept of nationalism.

There is no simple formulaic definition of Zionism. However, any articulation of Zionism, such as the one above by Malcolm Hedding, must express, one way or another, the ideas that 1) the Jewish people are a distinct people; 2) like other peoples, Jews are, and

Jewishness is, best actualized in a nation-state characterized by national institutions and distinct boundaries; and 3) that this organization into a nation-state is not only a political and historical necessity, but a moral imperative as well. None of these essentials is unambiguous and none is beyond question, but whenever you find these ingredients, you will find a Zionist, whether he or she is Christian or Jewish, religious or secular, fundamentalist or progressive. When one considers these three characteristic features—each of which involves elaborate corollaries—one begins to get a feel for *mainstream* Zionism in contradistinction to *fundamentalist* Zionism. These three characteristics—that for the Jewish people, the establishment of the State of Israel is both a political necessity and a moral imperative—are common to those who identify themselves as Zionists.

Where do we find exponents of Zionism, so defined, among mainstream Christians? Let's start with Reinhold Niebuhr, the iconic Protestant liberal Christian. Niebuhr was educated at Yale and wrote prolifically for the *Christian Century*, the *Nation,* the *New Republic*, and his own *Christianity in Crisis*. He was eventually appointed professor of ethics at Union Theological Seminary. He was by no means a fundamentalist. There is no hint of any reference to the fulfilment of biblical prophecy in his writings. Indeed, he denigrates such views. Niebuhr's unwavering support for Jewish causes was nurtured by strong *philo-Judaism*. He was motivated not by restorationist theology and informed not by biblical literalism, but by moral outrage over the experience of Jews in Nazi Germany and throughout Europe and central Asia. For him, support for the Jewish people required support for the Jewish state and both were moral imperatives. His conscience was attuned to issues of justice and the moral obligation of Christians to respond to social challenges. He spoke frequently in support of Zionism to Jewish audiences. Leaders of Zionist organizations identified him as one who could be counted on to advance their agenda among Christians and he agreed to write a two-part pro-Zionist article that appeared in *The Nation.* He wrote:

> The problem of what is to become of the Jews in the postwar world ought to engage all of us, not only because a suffering people has a claim upon our compassion but because the very quality of our civilization is involved in the solution... The Jews require a homeland...[1]

---

[1] Merkley, *Christian Attitudes*, 137.

Clearly, Niebuhr was predisposed by his theological orientation toward empathy for Jews. Just as clearly, he had no interest in fundamentalist biblical hermeneutics. Does that fact alone, however, disqualify him from the ranks of Zionists? On the contrary, his orientation toward Zionism perfectly illustrates that fundamentalism is not a precondition for Christian Zionism. He wrote:

> Many Christians are pro-Zionist in the sense that they believe that a homeless people require a homeland; but we feel as embarrassed as anti-Zionist religious Jews when messianic claims are used to substantiate the right of the Jews to the particular homeland in Palestine... History is full of strange configurations. Among them is the thrilling emergence of the State of Israel.[1]

Zionism and the Mainstream Academy

Turning to the arena of Christian biblical scholarship, Christian Zionism is ubiquitous. In recent years, prominent biblical scholars, including Keith Whitelam, Thomas Thompson, and Michael Prior have produced groundbreaking works demonstrating that both biblical archaeology and the broader field of biblical studies are dominated by scholars whose ideas

---

[1] Merkley, *Christian Attitudes*, 141.

are sympathetic to and have the effect of validating the Zionist enterprise.[1] This is particularly obvious when one travels through Israel, where virtually every archaeological endeavor is pressed into Zionist service to reinforce the Zionist narrative of Jewish return and validate exclusive Jewish claims to the land.

Neil Asher Silberman explores this theme vigorously as it pertains to Zionist historiography.[2] One outstanding example, among many, is the

---

[1] See, e.g., Keith W. Whitelam, *The Invention of Ancient Israel: The Silencing of Palestinian History* (Rev. ed.; New York: Routledge, 1997); Keith W. Whitelam and Robert B. Coote, eds., *The Emergence of Early Israel in Historical Perspective* (Sheffield: Sheffield Phoenix, 2010); Keith W. Whitelam and Emanuel Pfoh, eds., *The Politics of Israel's Past: The Bible, Archaeology and Nation-Building* (Sheffield: Sheffield Phoenix, 2013); Keith W. Whitelam, *Holy Land as Homeland? Models for Constructing the Historic Landscapes of Jesus* (Sheffield: Sheffield Phoenix, 2011); Michael Prior, *Holy Land, Hollow Jubilee: God, Justice, and the Palestinians* (Bethlehem: Sabeel, 1999); *Zionism and the State of Israel: A Moral Inquiry* (New York: Routledge, 1999); *The Bible and Colonialism: A Moral Critique* (Sheffield: Sheffield Academic, 1997); Thomas L. Thompson, *The Mythic Past: Biblical Archaeology and the Myth of Israel* (New York: Basic Books, 2008); *Early History of the Israelite People: From the Written and Archaeological Sources* (Leiden: Brill, 1992); and *Biblical Narrative and Palestine's History* (Rev. ed.; Changing Perspectives 2; New York: Routledge, 2014).*

[2] Neil Asher Silberman, *Between Past and Present: Archaeology, Ideology, and Nationalism in the Modern Middle East* (New York: H. Holt, 1989).*

archaeological excavation of Masada. Yigal Yadin, an avowed Zionist who directed the dig and who first published its findings, is the author of the popular myth of Masada. Yadin's findings and the Masada story were subsequently debunked, but, nevertheless, live on because they fit so well with the worldview of contemporary Israelis.[1] Twenty-five years after Silberman published his work, Christian pilgrims, no less than Israeli school groups, are saturated with the fiction of Jewish Zealots heroically defying overwhelming odds, just as the Israeli Defense Force is said to do today in its aggressive wars of "self-defense." Biblical scholars reinforce this link by happily adopting Zionist language of Jewish return to the land. That Jesus and his compatriots, both those who were his supporters and those who were his detractors, belonged to one unified *Jewish people* is almost uncontested in biblical scholarship. English translations of the New Testament routinely refer to Jesus, his followers, and his opponents all as *Jews*, even

---

[1] See, for example, Nachman ben-Yehuda, *The Masada Myth: Collective Memory and Mythmaking in Israel* (Madison: University of Wisconsin Press, 1995) and *Sacrificing Truth: Archaeology and the Myth of Masada* (Amherst: Prometheus, 2002).*

though careful translation of the original languages of the texts would call for more nuanced translation.[1]

Just as astonishingly, modern biblical scholars constantly refer to Jesus or Paul as practitioners of *Judaism* without nuance. The diversity of conceptions implied by the Greek noun *Ioudaios* and its cognates is consistently undermined in contemporary Biblical translations. In fact, the contrast between the scarcity of the unnuanced references to *Judaism* in first-century literature and its frequency in contemporary biblical scholarship is striking and well illustrates the degree to which mainstream Christian biblical scholarship helps to cement the connection between modern Zionist Jews and their claim to the territory of ancient Israel. Interpretation matters. Words not only describe reality. Words also condition the way we think about reality. The words biblical scholars use to describe the ancient past promotes an identification of modern Jews with ancient Jews and reinforces the Zionist claim of a direct line between past and present and the natural return of the Jews to their ancestral land. It should be observed that the archaeologists and

---

[1] See Peter Miano, "The Biblical Academy and Christian anti-Semitism." *Newsletter of the Society for Biblical Studies* 14.2 (October 2015): 2, 6–8. Available online at: http://www.sbsedu. org/L3_e_newsletter10.15.pdf (accessed 6/29/16).*

historians whose historiographies are so harmonious with the Zionist enterprise, more often than not, are Christians who are neither fundamentalist nor dispensationalist.

Zionist ideology depends heavily on the idea of a distinct modern ethnic group which originated in the territory of ancient Israel and which can trace an uninterrupted lineage to ancient Israel. This historical oversimplification undergirds many modern Zionist claims to the contemporary real estate in Palestine. Such Zionism appeals to biblical archaeology to validate its contemporary claims to ethnic identity and territorial integrity. But the scholarship is not merely congenial to Zionist ideology. Biblical scholars themselves often uncritically presume the ethnic identity, territorial legitimacy, and nationalist aspirations at the root of Zionism. If the assumptions of the scholars are identical with those of Zionists, why do we not consider those scholars Zionists?

Mainstream Christian Zionism also pervades one of the most hallowed precincts of liberal, mainstream Christianity, namely so-called Jewish-Christian dialogue. It is no surprise that Jews involved in the dialogue display obvious Zionist sympathies, but their Christian counterparts are often equally and unapologetically Zionist. It is also in this realm that the challenges associated with identifying and critiquing mainstream Christian Zionism are most apparent. Unlike the ranks of fundamentalist Christian Zionists, whose opinions are often shrugged off as "lunatic ravings," mainstream Christian Zionists are not easy targets. Not only does mainstream Christian Zionism include icons of liberal, progressive Christianity, their motivation for assuming obviously Zionist positions is motivated by and grounded in sincere moral concern.

The reality of Jewish suffering should be prominent in all Christian thinking, but in the formal circles of Jewish-Christian dialogue, it propels Christian participants to adopt clearly Zionist positions.[1] Almost without exception, their concern grows out of sincere regard for Jewish suffering and the demands of justice and restitution. Rarely, however, does their concern extend equally to the Palestinians who experience Zionism as an instrument of catastrophe. One notable example among many is Father Robert Drinan, formerly Dean of the School of Law at Boston College and professor of law at Georgetown University. Drinan was a well-known activist in liberal social causes throughout his long and illustrious career. However, in

---

[1] For a detailed critique of this practice, see, for example, Michael Prior, *Zionism and the State of Israel*.

describing Zionism, Drinan uses language that would have surprised even Herzl, whom, he says, pursued his "messianic pilgrimage" with a zeal "infused with a compelling humanitarianism combined with traces of Jewish mysticism." The "mystery" and "majesty" of Zionism appears in its glory from Herzl's tomb. Now that the state is established, Christians should support it "in reparation or restitution for the genocide of Jews carried out in a nation whose population was overwhelmingly Christian."[1] Let's not ignore Father Drinan's distinguished ten-year career as a member of the US House of Representatives (Democrat-Massachusetts), during which he had numerous opportunities to express his enthusiasm for Zionism by voting in favor of legislation and resolutions that were staunchly pro-Israel. He is, thus, also an example of the way in which mainstream Christian Zionism pervades US political institutions.

Conclusion

Very few topics generate fervent debate, arouse passions, and evoke confusion like the Israeli-Palestinian conflict. This is because it veers into the

---

[1] Robert F. Drinan, *Honor the Promise: America's Commitment to Israel* (New York: Doubleday, 2007), 32, 39, 1.

volatile areas of religion and politics. Personal faith, interpretation of scripture, personal loyalties, moral convictions, and deeply-held political opinions overlap and collide in a confused sea of facts, perceptions, images, and realities. Notwithstanding these treacherous emotional waters, conscientious American Christians have no choice but to attempt to navigate them, because their churches and their government are both deeply complicit in the sadness and suffering of the people of Israel and Palestine.

In spite of the often repeated critiques of fundamentalist Christian Zionism, a more pervasive, pernicious, and sophisticated form of Zionism has been overlooked. I call it *mainstream Christian Zionism*. I believe that most American Christians should be included in this category. But if only half of mainstream American Christians are Zionists, then mainstream Christian Zionists outnumber American Jewish Zionists by 14:1.[1] Were it not for this form of Christian Zionism, the more easily identifiable, easily critiqued, unsophisticated form of Christian Zionism would not have the effect that it has. The minority wields great influence and exerts great energy, but they still need

---

[1] 157 million mainstream Christians/2 = 75 million : 5.5 million Jewish Americans

the majority to effect policy and the majority is only too happy to play its part. Mainstream Christian Zionism does not depend on biblical authority for its legitimacy. It is rooted in genuine moral sensitivities. Its appeal is to moral imperatives and political necessity rather than personal piety. It assumes uncritically that nationalism is natural and necessary and so starts with a predisposition to Jewish nationalism. It is far better organized, far better funded, and far more politically potent than its fundamentalist cousin.

Reconsidering Christian Zionism in its mainstream form leads inevitably to vexing moral conflicts. It requires re-examination of widely held assumptions about ethnic identity and nationhood and the moral implications of these. It raises issues that are considered taboo in the Church and takes us into perilous moral and academic "no-fly zones." But intellectual honesty requires no less.

It is, of course, quite convenient for mainstream Christians to identify Christian Zionism exclusively with evangelical, fundamentalist Christians. It is always easier to identify other people's defects than one's own. Mark Twain reportedly once said, "Nothing so needs reforming as other people's habits." Jesus said, "First take the log out of your own eye…"

Mainstream, liberal Christians cannot absolve themselves of complicity in the Zionist enterprise simply because they are not fundamentalists. If they espouse views that are identical to the nationalist assumptions of self-confessed secular and religious Jewish Zionists, then they themselves should be identified as Zionists.

Equating Christian Zionism so thoroughly with evangelical, fundamentalist Christians, or with the Christian right, is highly misleading, and ignores the reality that Christian Zionist support for the State of Israel comes overwhelmingly from mainstream Christians. Until we understand Christian Zionism in its *mainstream* aspects, however, we have not begun to appreciate how pervasive—and, therefore, how dangerous—Zionism really is.

Contributors

Mark Braverman is a clinical psychologist with a distinguished practice in the prevention of violence and the treatment of violence-induced trauma. Dr. Braverman is also the founder of Kairos International and the author of numerous books and articles, including *A Wall in Jerusalem: Hope, Healing, and the Struggle for Justice in Israel and Palestine* (2013) and *Fatal Embrace: Christians, Jews, and the Search for Peace in the Holy Land* (2012).

Noam Chomsky is one of the world's leading linguists and civil rights activists. Dr. Chomsky served as a professor at the Massachusetts Institute of Technology from 1955 until his retirement in 2005. Chomsky has authored hundreds of books and articles, including *American Power and the New Mandarins* (1969), *Peace in the Middle East?* (1974), *Manufacturing Consent: The Political Economy of the Mass Media* (with Edward S. Herman, 1988), *Profit over People* (1998), *Rogue States* (2000), *Gaza in Crisis* (with Ilan Pappe, 2010), and *On Western Terrorism: From Hiroshima to Drone Warfare* (2013).

Peter Miano is the executive director of the Society for Biblical Studies. He has earned advanced degrees in New Testament and missiology at Union Theological Seminary (New York City), Harvard Divinity School, and Boston University School of Theology. Rev. Miano is the author of *The Word of God and the World of the Bible: An Introduction to the Cultural Backgrounds of the New Testament* (2001).

Ilan Pappe is Professor of History and Director of the European Centre for Palestine Studies and International Studies at the University of Exeter in the United Kingdom. Pappe was born in Haifa, Israel. He served as a senior lecturer in political science at the University of Haifa (1984–2007) and chair of the Emil Touma Institute for Palestinian and Israeli Studies in Haifa (2000–2008). He is the author of *The Ethnic Cleansing of Palestine* (2006), *The Modern Middle East* (2005), *A History of Modern Palestine: One Land, Two Peoples* (2003), and *Britain and the Arab-Israeli Conflict* (1988).

Thomas E. Phillips is Professor of Theological Bibliography and New Testament at Claremont School of Theology. Dr. Phillips is the former chair of the Section on Acts at the Society of Biblical Literature and the lead translator for the Gospel of Luke in the *Common English Bible*. Dr. Phillips is the author or editor of scores of scholarly books and articles, including *Acts in Diverse Frames of Reference* (2009), *Reading Acts Today* (2011), and *Paul, His Letters and Acts* (2009).

Sara Roy is a senior research scholar at the Center for Middle Eastern Studies at Harvard University, specializing in the Palestinian economy, Palestinian Islamism, and the Israeli-Palestinian conflict. Dr. Roy is co-chair of the Middle East Seminar, jointly sponsored by the Weatherhead Center for International Affairs and the Center for Middle Eastern Studies, and co-chair of the Middle East Forum at the Center for Middle Eastern Studies. Dr. Roy has authored over 100 publications dealing with Palestinian issues and the Israeli-Palestinian conflict, and has lectured widely in the United States, Europe, the Middle East, and Australia.

Stephen M. Walt is the Robert and Renee Belfer Professor of International Affairs at Harvard University. He previously taught at Princeton University and the University of Chicago. He has been a Resident Associate of the Carnegie Endowment for Peace and a Guest Scholar at the Brookings Institution. He has also served as a consultant for the Institute of Defense Analyses, the Center for Naval Analyses, and the National Defense University. He presently serves on the editorial boards of several leading scholarly journals and he is the author of *The Origins of Alliances* (1987), which received the 1988 Edgar S. Furniss National Security Book Award. He is also the author of *Revolution and War* (1996), *Taming American Power: The Global Response to U.S. Primacy* (2005), and, with co-author J. J. Mearsheimer, *The Israel Lobby* (2007).

Jean Zaru is active in leadership at the Ramallah Friends Meeting in Palestine. She serves as an instructor for religion and ethics at the Friends Schools in Ramallah. Ms. Zaru served as a member of the Central Committee of the World Council of Churches from 1975–1983 and she is a founding member of Sabeel, an ecumenical study center for Palestinian Liberation Theology. She is the author of *A Christian Palestinian Life: Faith and Struggle* (2004), *Structural Violence: Truth and Peace-Keeping in the Palestinian Experience* (2004), and *Occupied with Non-Violence: A Palestinian Woman Speaks* (2008).

Bibliography

Alcalay, Ammiel. *Memories of Our Future: Selected Essays 1982–1999.* Los Angeles: Skylights Press, 2001.

Arendt, Hannah. *The Origins of Totalitarianism.* New York: Harcourt, Brace, Jovanovich, 1973.

Ben Ami, Shlomo. *Scars of War, Wounds of Peace: The Israeli-Arab Tragedy.* New York: Oxford University Press, 2007.

Ben-Yehuda, Nachman. *The Masada Myth: Collective Memory and Mythmaking in Israel.* Madison: University of Wisconsin Press, 1995.

_____. *Sacrificing Truth: Archaeology and the Myth of Masada.* Amherst: Prometheus, 2002.

Braverman, Mark. *Fatal Embrace: Christians, Jews, and the Search for Peace in the Holy Land.* New York: Beaufort Books, 2012.

_____. *Preventing Workplace Violence: A Guide for Employers and Practitioners.* Advanced Topics in Organizational Behavior. New York: Sage, 1998.

_____. *A Wall in Jerusalem: Hope, Healing, and the Struggle for Justice in Israel and Palestine.* Nashville: Jericho Books, 2013.

Brown, Robert McAfee. *Kairos: Three Prophetic Challenges to the Church.* Grand Rapids: Eerdmans, 1990.

Brueggemann, Walter. *Theology of the Old Testament: Testimony, Dispute, Advocacy.* Minneapolis: Fortress Press, 2005.

Culver, Douglas Joel. "The Contribution of Sir Henry Finch (1558–1625) to British Nonconformist Eschatology: A Study in the Organic Character and Significance of the Doctrine of National Jewish Restoration to Palestine in the Historical Context of Time." Th.M. Thesis. Trinity Evangelical Divinity School, 1973.

de Gruchy, John W., ed. *Dietrich Bonhoeffer: Witness to Jesus Christ*. Making of Modern Theology. San Francisco: Collins, 1988.

_____. "Towards a Confessing Church." *Apartheid is a Heresy*, 75–93. Edited by John de Gruchy and Charles Villa-Vicencio. Grand Rapids: Eerdmans, 1983.

Drinan, Robert F. *Honor the Promise: America's Commitment to Israel*. New York: Doubleday, 2007.

Ellis, Marc H. *Israel and Palestine—Out of the Ashes: The Search for Jewish Identity in the Twenty-First Century*. London: Pluto Press, 2001.

_____. *Practicing Exile*. Minneapolis: Fortress, 2002.

Fawcett, Louise. *The International Relations of the Middle East*. New York: Oxford University Press, 2005.

Finch, Henry. *The World's Resurrection or The Calling of the Jewes: A Present to Judah and the Children of Israel that Ioyned with Him, and to Ioseph (That Valiant Tribe of Ephraim) and all the House of Israel that Ioyned with Him*. London: Edward Griffin for William Bladen, 1621.

Finkielkraut, Alain. "A Pair of Boots is as Good as Shakespeare." *Education in France: Continuity and Change in the Mitterand Years 1981–95*, 327–34. Edited by Anne Corbert and Bob Moon. New York: Routledge, 2004.

Frye, Northrop. "The Knowledge of Good and Evil." *The Morality of Scholarship*, 1–28. Edited by Max Black. Ithaca: Cornell University Press, 1967.

Hoodbhoy, Pervez and Zia Main, "Nuclear Fears, Hopes and Realities in Pakistan." *International Affairs* 90.5 (2014): 1125–42.

Horowitz, Adam, Lizzy Ratner and Philip Weiss, eds. *The Goldstone Report: The Legacy of the Landmark Investigation of the Gaza Conflict*. New York: Nations Books, 2011.

Huntington, Samuel. "Why International Primacy Matters." *International Security* 17.4 (Spring 1993): 68-83.

Judt, Tony. "Israel: The Alternative." *The New York Review of Books*. New York: NYREV, Inc., October 23, 2003.

Ka-Tzetnik 135633. *Shivitti: A Vision*. San Francisco: Harper & Row, 1989.

Klepfisz, Irena. "Yom Hashoah, Yom Yerushalayim: A Meditation." *Dreams of an Insomniac: Jewish Feminist Essays, Speeches and Diatribes*, 115–40. Portland, OR: Eighth Mountain Press, 1980.

Klug, Francesca. "Speaking Out for Human Rights." *Jewish Quarterly* 61.3–4 (2014): 74.

LaHaye, Tim and Jerry B. Jenkins. *Left Behind*. Carol Stream, IL: Tyndale House Publishers, 1995.

Lessing, Doris. *Prisons We Choose to Live Inside*. Milton, PA: Flamingo Press, 1993.

Mearsheimer, John J. and Stephen M. Walt. *The Israel Lobby and U.S. Foreign Policy*. New York: Farrar, Straus and Giroux, 2007.

Miano, Peter. "The Biblical Academy and Christian anti-Semitism." *Newsletter of the Society for Biblical Studies* 14.2 (October 2015): 2, 6–8.

_____. "Mainstream Christian Zionism." *Speaking the Truth: Zionism, Israel and Occupation*, 126–47. Edited by Michael Prior. London: Melisende, 2004.

_____. *The Word of God and the World of the Bible: An Introduction to the Cultural Backgrounds of the New Testament*. London: Melisende, 2001.

Merkley, Paul. *Christian Attitudes towards the State of Israel*. Montreal: McGill-Queen's University Press, 2007.

Orwell, George. *Animal Farm*. New York: Signet, 1946.

Pappe, Ilan. *The Biggest Prison on Earth: A History of the Occupied Territories*. New York: OneWorld Publications, 2016.

_____. *The Ethnic Cleansing of Palestine*. Reprint ed. New York: OneWorld Publications, 2007.

_____. *The Forgotten Palestinians: A History of the Palestinians in Israel*. New Haven: Yale University Press, 2013.

_____. *A History of Modern Palestine: One Land, Two Peoples.* Paperback ed. Cambridge: Cambridge University Press, 2006.

_____. *The Idea of Israel: A History of Power and Knowledge*. London: Verso, 2016.

_____. *Israel and South Africa: The Many Faces of Apartheid*. London: Zed Books, 2015.

_____. *The Modern Middle East: A Social and Cultural History.* 3rd Edition. New York: Routledge, 2014.

_____. *The Making of the Arab-Israeli Conflict, 1947–1951*. Rev. ed. London: I. B. Tauris, 2014.

_____. *Out of the Frame: The Struggle for Academic Freedom in Israel*. London: Pluto Press, 2010.

_____. *The Rise and Fall of a Palestinian Dynasty: The Husaynis, 1700–1948*. Los Angeles: University of California Press, 2011.

Paas, Steven. Christian Zionism Examined: A Review of *Ideas on Israel, the Church and the Kingdom*. Nuremberg: VTR Publications, 2012.

Pollack, Kenneth M., Daniel L. Byman, Martin Indyk, Suzanne Maloney, Michael E. O'Hanlon and Bruce Riedel. "Which Path to Persia? Options for a New American Strategy toward Iran." *Analysis Paper* 20. Washington, DC: Saban Center for Middle East Policy at the Brookings Institution, 2009.

Prior, Michael. *The Bible and Colonialism: A Moral Critique*. Sheffield: Sheffield Academic, 1997.

_____. *Holy Land, Hollow Jubilee: God, Justice, and the Palestinians*. Bethlehem: Sabeel, 1999.

_____. *Zionism and the State of Israel: A Moral Inquiry*. New York: Routledge, 1999.

Rose, Jacqueline. *The Last Resistance*. New York: Verso, 2007.

Roy, Sara. *Failing Peace: Gaza and the Palestinian-Israeli Conflict*. London: Pluto Press, 2007.

_____. "Gaza: No se puede mirar—One Cannot Look"— A Brief Reflection." *Gaza as Metaphor*, 219–24. Edited by Helga Tawil-Souri and Dina Matar. London: Hurst, 2016.

_____. *The Gaza Strip: The Political Economy of De-development*. 3rd ed. Washington, DC: Institute for Palestine Studies, 2015.

_____. *Hamas and Civil Society in Gaza: Engaging the Islamist Social Sector*. Princeton Studies in Muslim Politics. Princeton: Princeton University Press, 2013.

_____. "A Jewish Plea." *The War on Lebanon: A Reader*, 302–13. Edited by Nubar Hovsepian. Northampton, MA: Olive Branch Press, 2008.

_____. "Living with the Holocaust: The Journey of a Child of Holocaust Survivors." *Journal of Palestine Studies* 32.1 (Autumn 2002): 5–12.

Said, Edward. *Humanism and Democratic Criticism*. New York: Columbia University Press, 2004.

_____. *Representations of the Intellectual: The 1993 Reith Lectures.* New York: Vintage, 1996.

Samore, Gary, ed. *Iran's Strategic Weapons Programmes: A Net Assessment*. International Institute for Strategic Studies. New York: Routledge, 2005.

Shakespeare, William. *King Lear*. Edited by Joseph Pearce. Ignatius Critical Editions. San Francisco: Ignatius Press, 2008.

Silberman, Neil Asher. *Between Past and Present: Archaeology, Ideology, and Nationalism in the Modern Middle East*. New York: H. Holt, 1989.

Sizer, Stephen. *Challenging Christian Zionism: Theology, Politics and the Israel-Palestine Conflict*. London: Melisende, 2005.

_____. *Christian Zionism: Road Map to Armageddon?* Downers Grove, IL: IVP Academic, 2006.

Thompson, Thomas L. *Biblical Narrative and Palestine's History*. Rev. ed. Changing Perspectives 2. New York: Routledge, 2014.

_____. *Early History of the Israelite People: From the Written and Archaeological Sources*. Leiden: Brill, 1992.

_____. *The Mythic Past: Biblical Archaeology and the Myth of Israel*. New York: Basic Books, 2008.

Villa-Vicencio, Charles. *Trapped in Apartheid*. Maryknoll, NY: Orbis, 1988.

Walt, Stephen. *The Origins of Alliance*. Cornell Studies in Security Affairs. Ithaca: Cornell University Press, 1990.

_____. *Revolution and War*. Cornell Studies in Security Affairs. Ithaca: Cornell University Press, 1997.

_____. *Taming American Power: The Global Response to U.S. Primacy*. New York: Norton, 2006.

Weschler, Lawrence. *A Miracle, a Universe: Settling Scores with Torturers*. Chicago: University of Chicago Press, 1990.

_____. "A Miracle, a Universe: Settling Accounts with Torturers." *Transitional Justice: How Emerging Democracies Reckon with Former Regimes*, 1: 491–99. Edited by Neil J. Kritz. Washington, DC: United States Institute of Peace, 1995.

Whitelam, Keith W. *The Invention of Ancient Israel: The Silencing of Palestinian History*. Rev. ed. New York: Routledge, 1997.

_____. *Holy Land as Homeland? Models for Constructing the Historic Landscapes of Jesus*. Sheffield: Sheffield Phoenix, 2011.

Whitelam, Keith W. and Robert B. Coote, eds. *The Emergence of Early Israel in Historical Perspective*. Sheffield: Sheffield Phoenix, 2010.

Whitelam, Keith W. and Emanuel Pfoh, eds. *The Politics of Israel's Past: The Bible, Archaeology and Nation-Building*. Sheffield: Sheffield Phoenix, 2013.

Zaru, Jean. *Occupied with Nonviolence: A Palestinian Woman Speaks*. Minneapolis: Fortress, 2008.

Author Index

CPSIA information can be obtained
at www.ICGtesting.com
Printed in the USA
LVOW13s1019081216
516386LV00014B/410/P